Rhema-Faith Ministries International

DISCOVERING GOD'S GIFTS TO THE CHURCH

The Holy Spirit and His Gifts

DR. BRIAN E. W. CRETTER

WESTBOW
PRESS®
A DIVISION OF THOMAS NELSON
& ZONDERVAN

WestBow Press books may be ordered through booksellers or by contacting:

WestBow Press
A Division of Thomas Nelson & Zondervan
1663 Liberty Drive
Bloomington, IN 47403
www.westbowpress.com
1 (866) 928-1240

ISBN: 978-1-9736-0372-6 (sc)
ISBN: 978-1-9736-0371-9 (hc)
ISBN: 978-1-9736-0373-3 (e)

Library of Congress Control Number: 2017914095

Print information available on the last page.

WestBow Press rev. date: 9/20/2017

Scripture taken from the King James Version of the Bible.

The Effect of the Holy Spirit and the Works of the Holy Spirit is taken from Chafer, Lewis Sperry, and John Walvoord, *Major Bible Themes* (Grand Rapids, MI: Zondervan, 1974). Used by permission of Zondervan.

The definition of the word *pastor* taken from Vine, W. E., Merrill F. Unger, and William White Jr., *Vine's Complete Expository Dictionary of Old and New Testament Words* (Nashville: Thomas Nelson, 1985), 462. Used by permission of Thomas Nelson.

The definition of the word *rhema* taken from W. E. *Vine's Expository Dictionary of the New Testament Words,* unbridged ed. (Maclean, VA: Macdonald Publishing), 1253. Used by permission of Macdonald Publishing.

The section Types of Apostles was taken from Dr. Bill Hamon, *Apostles, Prophets and the Coming Moves of God,* Different Types of Apostles pages 223–227 (Destiny Image Publishers, Inc. Shippensburg, PA. 17257-0310, 1997), Reproduced by permission of Destiny Image Publishers, Inc.

CONTENTS

INTRODUCTION

People of the church today desire to explore what their purpose is in the body of Christ. There is a purpose for everyone in the body of Christ. First and foremost, the Lord wants us to spread the gospel by way of visiting those in prison and those who are sick, clothing the naked, feeding the hungry, and making provision for the homeless (Matt. 25:35–40). These forms of ministry give opportunities to tell the good news.

Many people in the body of Christ assume one must be a preacher or pastor to do ministry, but that isn't so. Leadership or the fivefold ministry, as listed in Ephesians 4:11–13, isn't for everyone. The purpose of the ministry gifts is to equip the saint for the work of the ministry and maturity until there is unity of the faith and knowledge of the Son of God. Therefore, as individuals are equipped for the work of the ministry, the operation of the gifts of the Holy Spirit can and will be manifested in their lives.

The purpose of this book is that you will pray about and discover your spiritual gift or gifts. Every gift is an important one. The gifts in operation behind the scenes, such as the gift of helps, are just as important as the office of the apostle.

The gifts in this book are listed in five categories: revelation gifts, power gifts, vocal gifts, and auxiliary gifts—and then the fivefold ministry gifts. One's desire for any gift should be coupled with prayer and faith. As we believe the Lord Jesus Christ for certain gifts, we can accomplish the great commission He has given us to do, to go into all the world and make disciples of all nations. We have to believe God for the work and kingdom building. Jesus said in Mark 16:17–18, "And these signs shall follow them that believe; In my name shall they cast out devils; they shall speak with new tongues; They shall take up serpents; and if they drink any deadly thing, it shall not hurt them; they shall lay hands on the sick, and they shall recover." If we dare to believe and have faith in Christ's power to come through us and not depend on our own power, these gifts shall be ours. Pray, believe, receive, and watch God work through you and get the glory out of your life.

CHAPTER 1
The Holy Spirit Is God

> But Peter said, Ananias, why hath Satan filled thine heart to lie to the Holy Ghost? . . . why hast thou conceived this thing in thine heart? thou hast not lied unto men, but unto God. (Act 5:3-4)

In many cases, people think of the Holy Spirit as a mere influence or power. Some may question who the Holy Spirit is and what influence He has. The Holy Spirit is a divine person. He is holy and has all the attributes of the other two persons of the Godhead, God the Father and God the Son. As the third person of the Trinity, the Holy Spirit knows the purpose and plan of God the Father (1 Cor. 2:10–13). He has sensibilities (Rom. 8:27; 15:30; Eph. 4:30) and will (1 Cor. 12: 11; Heb. 2:4). He is equal to God the Father and God the Son. Therefore, He is God, God the Holy Spirit.

> And the earth was without form, and void; and darkness was upon the face of the deep. And the Spirit of God moved upon the face of the waters. (Gen. 1:2)

> And God said, "Let us make man in our image, after our likeness." (Gen. 1:26)

> Go ye therefore and teach all nations, baptizing
> them in the name of the Father and of the Son
> and of the Holy Ghost. (Matt. 28:19)

God the Holy Spirit shouldn't be taken lightly. He isn't any holier than God the Father or God the Son. Holiness is their primary attribute (see Phil. 2:5–7; 2 Cor. 3:8, 17). When we commune with the Holy Spirit, we commune with God. The Holy Spirit is the spirit of God the Son, Jesus Christ. Galatians 4:6 says, "And because ye are sons, God hath sent forth the Spirit of his Son into your hearts, crying, Abba, Father."

The Holy Spirit speaks not of Himself but of Jesus Christ, God the Son. He speaks the will of Christ, and Christ knows the will of God the Father. So when we hear from God the Holy Spirit, we hear from God. John 16:13–15 says, "Howbeit when he, the Spirit of truth is come he will guide you into all truth: for he shall not speak of himself; but whatsoever he shall hear, that shall he speak: and he will show you things to come. He shall glorify me: for he shall receive of mine, and shall show it unto you. All things that the Father hath are mine: therefore said I, that he shall take of mine, and shall show it unto you."

The Holy Spirit is sensitive to the needs and voice of both God and humans. We commune intimately with God through the Holy Spirit, and He communicates with us through the will of God the Father. We receive from God the Father through Christ Jesus and by the Holy Spirit. The believer can influence the Holy Spirit. The following are examples of how the believer can do so:

1. Tempt or test (Acts 5:9)
2. Lie to (Acts 5:37)
3. Grieve (Isa. 63:10; Eph. 4:30)
4. Resist (Acts 7:51)
5. Quench (1 Thess. 5:19)
6. Disrespect (Heb. 10:29)

7. Blaspheme (Matt.12:31)
8. Speak against (Matt. 12:32)
9. Distinguish from one's own thoughts (Acts 10:38; 1 Cor. 2:4)

Romans 8:26 says, "Likewise the Spirit also helpeth our infirmities: for we know not what we should pray for as we ought: but the Spirit itself maketh intercession for us with groanings which cannot be uttered." Yes, the Holy Spirit prays and intercedes on our behalf when the cares of this world and the deep concerns of our hearts overwhelm us. The Holy Spirit, who is within us, prays for us with words that are sometimes inexpressible.

The Holy Spirit existed before time and will do so after time has ended. He is eternal (Heb. 9:14), omniscient (1 Cor. 2:10–13; John 14:26; 16:12–15), and omnipresent (Ps. 139:7–10). The Holy Spirit is an object of our faith in experiencing the presence of God (Ps. 51:11). Because the Holy Spirit is God, we must obey Him (Acts 10:19–21).

When we walk in fellowship with the Holy Spirit, He guides and instructs us. We can therefore experience His power and sufficiency (John 14:26; Acts 2:2; 1 John 2:27).

What is the purpose of the Holy Spirit? When a person sincerely confesses a belief in Jesus Christ's death, burial, and resurrection, the Holy Spirit regenerates him or her. The word *regenerate* is defined as "to reform or to make new,"[1]

Regeneration is a supernatural act of God on man's confession of salvation. Regeneration isn't by works of man but is freely given to all who believe. The regeneration process begins at the moment of confession of salvation. The inner spirit is renewed or, as Jesus said, born again.

Titus 3:5 says, "Not by works of righteousness which we have

---

[1] The American Heritage Dictionary, Second College Edition © 1982, 1985 by Houghton Mifflin Company

done, but according to his mercy he saved us, by the washing of regeneration, and renewing of the Holy Ghost." (Also see Matt. 19:28; John 1:13; 5:21; Rom. 6:13; Eph. 2:5; 2 Cor. 5:17; 1 Peter 2:9).

John 3:4 says, "Jesus answered, and said unto him, Verily, verily, I say unto thee, Except a man be born again, he cannot see the kingdom of God." In regeneration, the spirit of man is brought to life. To be born again in the spirit by the Holy Spirit brings a conscious realization of God's ways and will for the believer. The regeneration process deals with the spirit and soul of the believer. The heart, emotions, and the intellect make up the soul, and the conscience and free will make up the inner man, the spirit man. The spirit part of a person looks vertically toward God, and the soul looks horizontally toward earth. The spirit is regenerated or born again, and the soul must be more submissive to the word, way, and will of God. This process is called "sanctification." The spirit brings forth a consciousness or awareness of God. The soul and spirit make up the true person and are manifested through the flesh.

Our minds must be reconditioned to think spiritually, not religiously. The mind is always wrestling between flesh and spirit. The word of God helps to purge our souls from uncleanness and grow to grow our spirits. If the believer applies the inspired scriptures to his or her life, this step will result in a closer walk with God.

> For the word of God is quick, and powerful, and sharper than any two-edged sword, piercing even to the dividing asunder of soul and spirit, and of the joints and marrow, and is a discerner of the thoughts and intents of the heart. (Heb. 4:12)

> And be not conformed to this world: but be ye transformed by the renewing of your mind, that ye may prove what is that good, and acceptable, and perfect will of God. (Rom. 12:2)

> Keep thy heart, with all diligence; for out of it are
> the issues of life. (Prov. 4:23)

All life situations and circumstances are stored in the heart. The heart is the seat of the soul. Throughout life, our hearts get bruised and even broken; therefore, we must protect them and trust God with our hearts. The Holy Spirit brings life to what was dead, the spirit of man.

> Jesus said unto him, Thou shalt love the Lord, thy
> God with all thy heart, and with all thy soul, and
> with all thy mind. (Matt. 22:37; also see Deut. 6:5).

> Even when we were dead in sins, hath quickened
> us together with Christ (by grace ye are saved).
> (Eph. 2:5)

Therefore, a new convert has a different attitude toward God and strives for the high call of God, which seeks to live right and righteously before God. Another purpose of the Holy Spirit is to reveal God's will to the believer and the world. The works and words of the Holy Spirit are the works and words of God. The Holy Spirit testifies of Christ and His works. Anything the Holy Spirit speaks or shows is that of Jesus Christ.

> Jesus said, "But when the Comforter is come,
> whom I will send unto you from the Father even
> the Spirit of truth, who proceedeth from the
> Father, he shall testify of me." (John 15:26–27)

> Howbeit, when he, the Spirit of truth, is come, he
> will guide you into all truth for he shall not speak
> of himself, but whatever he shall hear, that shall
> he speak; and he will show you things to come. He

shall glorify me; for he shall receive of mine, and shall show it unto you. (John 16:13–14)

The Holy Spirit testifies that Jesus Christ is the Son of God. He bears witness that the works and words of Jesus Christ are true. As we read and study the word of God, the Holy Spirit within us bears witness to the word of God. The Holy Spirit is true. Therefore, He will reveal what is true and false.

The Holy Spirit also has a purpose in the lives of unbelievers. He shall convict the world of sin, righteousness, and judgment. He reproves the world of sin by showing people what is right, wrong, or godly. He brings a word of encouragement to those who try to live righteously and brings judgment on those who live wickedly and evilly. God is no respecter of persons. He brings judgment on both the just and the unjust. John 16:8–11 says, "Jesus said, And when He (the Holy Spirit) is come, He will reprove the world of sin, and of righteousness, and of judgment: of sin, because they believe not on me; of righteousness, because I go to my Father, and ye see me no more; of judgment, because the prince of this world is judged."

The Holy Spirit guides believers into all truth. He guides us into the truth of God's word. Many people in our modern time are presenting false teachings about the word of God. The Holy Spirit reveals the mysteries of God's word because He knows the deep things of God. First Corinthians 2:10 says, "But God hath revealed them unto us by his Spirit for the Spirit searcheth all things, yea, the deep things of God."

The Holy Spirit reveals the truths of God's word and shows us the truths regarding different situations in our lives. He will guide us in making the right decisions in our lives. James 1:5 says, "If any of you lack wisdom, let him ask of God. Who giveth to all men liberally, and upbraideth not, and it shall be given him."

We should always pray for God's guidance before we make any kind of decisions. The Holy Spirit searches and knows the hearts of people. We must make our requests known to God (Phil. 4:6).

The Holy Spirit searches and knows God's plan for every individual. Believers must be in fellowship with God to receive the plan of God for their lives. Another purpose of the Holy Spirit is to teach us and bring to our remembrance what Jesus said and did. As we read and study the Holy Bible, the Holy Spirit reveals to us the meaning of what we have read. He will give us the application and illustration in our hearts. Therefore, when we apply the gospel to our lives as the living word of God, the Holy Spirit will bring to our remembrance what we have learned and lived. The Holy Spirit reveals the word of God according to the measure of faith and maturity. If a believer is spiritually immature, the Holy Spirit will reveal the milk of the word of God rather than the meat of the word. John 14:26 says, "But the Comforter, who is the Holy Spirit, whom the Father will send in my name, he shall teach you all things, and bring all things to your remembrance, whatever I have said unto you."

Upon one's confession of salvation, the Holy Spirit baptizes the believer. Whether a believer shows an external expression of the baptism of the Holy Spirit depends on the situation of the believer's life and how the believer receives the preached word and repents of his or her sins. Some people are emotional and can make an intelligent decision that they need a savior in their lives.

The scriptures clearly teach that the baptism of the Holy Spirit takes place at the moment of conversion. That's when the believer is baptized into the body of Christ and into Christ (1 Cor. 12:13; Gal. 3:27). There is scriptural evidence for an outward expression of the baptism of the Holy Spirit (for example, speaking in tongues and prophesying [Acts 2:4; 10:34–46; 19:2–6; 21:8]). However, a person's conversion isn't based on the outward expression of the baptism of the Holy Spirit. True evidence is a changed life. The Bible speaks not of seeking to be *baptized* in the Spirit but of being *filled* with the Spirit. Ephesians 5:18 says, "And be not drunk with wine, in which is excess, but be filled with the Spirit."

Baptism into the body of Christ initiates a new beginning

and environment for the new convert, who will have new friends and a spiritual family. The Spirit of God is constantly adding to the body of Christ. Once a person is in the body of Christ, he or she is equipped with various gifts of the Holy Spirit. Each believer has an opportunity to serve God and operate through the gifts of the Spirit within the framework of his or her own personality. At conversion, the believer is baptized into Christ and therefore has a new position in Him. We are identified with His death, burial, and resurrection. Christ is the head of the church. We have access to God the Father through Christ Jesus and by His Holy Spirit. Jesus Christ said in John 15:4, "Abide in me, and I in you. As the branch cannot bear fruit of itself, except it abide in the vine; no more can ye, except ye abide in me."

The baptism of the Holy Spirit brings about a continuous conscious realization of God's ways and desires. The baptism of the Holy Spirit brings about identification with Christ. Because the believer is identified with Christ, he or she is identified with the life and work of Christ. Romans 6:1–4 says, "What shall we say then? Shall we continue in sin that grace may abound? God forbid. How shall we, that are dead to sin, live any longer in it? Know ye not that, as many of us as were baptized into Jesus Christ were baptized into his death? Therefore, we are buried with him by baptism into death that as Christ was raised up from the dead by the glory of the Father; even so we also should walk in newness of life."

Because we believers are baptized into Christ, our hearts' desires should be to walk in the righteousness of God. We should strive to live in accordance with the word of God. Some Christians takes grace for granted. Many have the mindset that they can live in sin because they are saved, and God will forgive them. God forbid that believers have such actions and thoughts. Colossians 2:11 says, "In whom also ye are circumcised with the circumcision made without hands, in putting off the body of the sins of the flesh by the circumcision of Christ."

The baptism of the Holy Spirit into the body of Christ brings the union of true believers together. The baptism gives a new and abiding relationship with others. Therefore, then, true believers don't desire to fellowship with old worldly friends or do the things they once did. The Holy Spirit, therefore, is the one who increases the fellowship of believers. Acts 2:46–47 says, "And they, continuing daily with one accord in the temple, and breaking bread from house to House, did eat their meat with gladness and singleness of heart, Praising God, and having favor with all the people. And the Lord added to the church daily such as should be saved."

Every believer is a member of the body of Christ. In addition, every believer has a gift and function in the body. Believers must recognize the gifts the Holy Spirit has given to them (Rom. 12:3–8; 1 Cor. 12:27–28; Eph. 4:7–16). Therefore, upon the confession of salvation, the regeneration of the Spirit, the baptism of the Spirit, and the indwelling of the Spirit all happen simultaneously. Simply stated, the indwelling of the Holy Spirit is the Spirit of God residing inside the believer. This is where God communicate with us and we with Him. The Holy Spirit also seals us unto the day of redemption. Jesus promised in the Gospel of John that the Holy Spirit will be with us and in us. The indwelling of the Spirit or the Holy Spirit is the Spirit of the Lord.

> Now the Lord is that Spirit: and where the Spirit of the Lord is, there is liberty. (2 Cor. 3:17)

> Even the Spirit of truth; whom the world cannot receive. Because it seeth him not, neither knoweth him: but ye know him; for he dwelleth with you, and shall be in you. (John 14:17)

The indwelling of the Holy Spirit is important to the lives of believers; it establishes our relationship with God. God is a spirit, and the spirit part of us must grow in the likeness of God. The

Holy Spirit's dwelling on the inside of the believer brings forth the fruit of the Spirit. The fruit of the Spirit are Christlike attributes. God spoke through the apostle Paul in Romans 8:9: "But ye are not in the flesh, but in the Spirit, if so be that the Spirit of God dwell in you. Now if any man have not the Spirit of Christ, he is none of his." Galatians 5:22 says, "But the fruit of the Spirit is love, joy, peace, longsuffering, gentleness, goodness, faith, meekness, temperance: against such there is no law."

As we allow our spirits to grow, these attributes will be manifested increasingly. The indwelling of the Holy Spirit will reveal the spiritual application of the word of God. John 6:63 says, "Jesus said, 'It is the spirit that quickeneth; the flesh profiteth nothing: the words that I speak unto you, they are spirit, and they are life.'" When a person reads the word of God and thinks carnally or in the flesh, he or she will have a lack of understanding. The word of God is spiritual and therefore must be understood spiritually. The Holy Spirit is the only one who can bring spiritual understanding.

Before the day of Pentecost, the baptism of the Holy Spirit wasn't available to the believer. The Holy Spirit came on only certain people in the Old Testament. There are prophetic messages in the Old Testament that tell of this occurrence (Isa. 44:3; Joel 2:28). On the day of Pentecost, a host of Jews and Galileans were baptized with the Holy Spirit and fire. John the Baptist preached in the wilderness. In John 3:11, John the Baptist said, "I indeed baptize you with water unto repentance: but he that cometh after me is mightier than I, whose shoes I am not worthy to bear: he shall baptize you with the Holy Ghost, and with fire."

After the day of Pentecost, the Holy Spirit was available to all who believed on Jesus Christ. In the Old Testament, the ark of the covenant, which was in the temple, represented the presence of God. The anointment with oil in the Old Testament represented the presence of the Holy Spirit.

Only selected people in the Old Testament were indwelt with

the Holy Spirit and anointed with oil. The prophets, kings, and priests were anointed with oil for the task before them. In the New Testament and in the present age, the body of the believer is the temple where the presence of God dwells. First Corinthians 3:16 says, "Know ye not that ye are the temple of God, and that the Spirit of God dwelleth in you?"

Once we have been born again and indwelt with the Holy Spirit, we no longer belong to ourselves. As we desire to grow, we should be more submissive to the Spirit of God. To be submissive to the Holy Spirit, believers must open their hearts and minds to the Holy Spirit. The more we open ourselves to the Spirit, the more He will reveal God's way and will. The apostle Paul said in 1 Corinthians 6:19, "What? Know ye not that your body is the temple of the Holy Ghost which is in you, which ye have of God, and ye are not of your own?"

We are Christians, and therefore, we should be followers of Christ. God is our Father, and we are His children. Therefore, the indwelling of the Holy Spirit sanctifies or sets us apart for God. The indwelling of the Holy Spirit brings consciousness of what actions we must take to please God. The Spirit of God won't do the thinking for us. God has given us common sense to discern between good and evil, right and wrong (Heb. 5:14). In Romans 9:1, Paul said, "I say the truth in Christ, I lie not, my conscience also bearing me witness in the Holy Ghost."

We talk to God with our spirits or the inner man. Every believer should have some quiet time with God, the Holy Spirit. There are times when we should meditate on the word of God and pray. Ephesians 6:18 says, "Praying always with all prayer and supplication in the Spirit." Psalm 1:2 talks about the believer's delight in the word of God. "But his delight is in the law of the Lord, and in his law doth he meditate day and night." Often we seek to hear from the Lord, but some look in all the wrong places. Truly, God will send a *rhema* word from some significant other, but He will also speak to us.

Ephesians 3:14–16 says, "For this cause I bow my knees unto the Father of our Lord Jesus Christ, Of whom the whole family in heaven and earth is named, That he would grant you, according to the riches of his glory, to be strengthened with might by his Spirit in the inner man." The identification of this is by unction or urging in our inner witness. The unction or anointing comes to confirm and sometimes calls for an individual to do something. The unction and anointing come from within. The anointing isn't just an experience but the powerful presence of a person, and that person is the Holy Spirit.

First John 2:20… 27 says, "But ye have an unction from the Holy One, and ye know all things. But the anointing which ye have received of him abideth in you, and ye need not that any man teach you: but as the same anointing teacheth you of all things, and is truth and is no lie, and even as it hath taught you, ye shall abide in him." We must remember that the anointing is the empowerment of the Spirit of the Anointed One. We should refer to Him, the Holy Spirit, as "He" and not as a thing. He is God. Some people are more anointed than others, because of the tasks God has given them. Some believers open themselves to the workings of the Holy Spirit at different degrees. Some may submit more than others. The more a believer submits to the Holy Spirit, the greater the anointing will be. Romans 12:3 says, "For I say, through the grace given unto me, to every man that is among you, not to think of himself more highly than he ought to think; but to think soberly, according as God hath dealt to every man the measure of faith."

We can increase the movement or anointing of the Holy Spirit in our lives by reading the word of God, meditating on it, having a productive prayer life, and submitting to the Holy Spirit. Through these disciplines, we strengthen our spirits; thus, we can hear the voice of God more clearly.

The scriptures teach us about the voice of God. John the revelator spoke of His voice as thunder and many waters, Rev. 14:2.

The voice of God to Elijah was a small, still voice. Jesus addressed the Holy Spirit as He. Therefore, we can conclude that the voice of God is that small, still, masculine voice that speaks deep within us. That voice is like no other. The voice of God is peaceful. It causes no confusion. The voice of God comes to us with answers, questions, directions, and of course, scriptures. Anytime He does speak, it isn't a premeditated thought. It isn't a thought of our own or a thought of another. It bears witness with our spirits. We often refer to the voice of God by saying, "Something told me."

The voice of God is that inner masculine voice we so often ignore. Some of us get confused with the voice of God, our own voice, and the voice of another. There are a few rules to distinguish the voices.

1. The voice of God isn't a premeditated voice.
2. God speaks to our spirit or inner man.
3. Other voices come through ears to our minds.
4. Other voices cause confusion.

If the voice of God is spoken in our spirits or by a *rhema* word, the message will always be in line with His written word, the Logos. We all need to be more sensitive to the voice of God and hear it with clarity. In doing so, we can truly obey Him if we desire to. The Holy Spirit convicts the soul of the individual when the believer sins against God or his or her brother. Often the conviction of the Holy Spirit is ignored because of one's pride and selfish motives. God through His Spirit will burden the mind or conscience until repentance is made. There are still some who will ignore the truth of God's will. The confusion comes when the believer cannot discern the voice of God from that of another. John 10:27 says, "My sheep hear my voice, and I know them, and they follow me."

Jesus promised not to leave us comfortless and said He will be with us until the end of the world. Therefore, the indwelling Holy Spirit is the Spirit of the Lord. Those who believe in Jesus

Christ and submit themselves to the Holy Spirit will have the Spirit springing out of them like living water. We must learn to be conscious of the Spirit within us. Our minds sometimes are contrary to what our spirits receive and witness. What we think or have been traditionally taught can hinder us from moving into the spirit realm. The word of God will bear witness with our inner witness. John 7:38 says, "He that believeth on me, as the scripture hath said, out of his belly shall flow rivers of living water. But this spake he of the Spirit, which they that believe on him should receive: for the Holy Ghost was not yet given; because that Jesus was not yet glorified."

The Works of the Holy Spirit

1. He regenerates (John 3:5; 1 John 5:1).
2. He teaches (John 14:26; 16:13–16; 1 John 2:27; 1 Cor. 2:13; Ps. 25:9).
3. He bears witness (John 15:26; 1 John 5:6).
4. He convicts (John 16:8–11).
5. He seals (Eph. 4:30).
6. He baptizes (1 Cor. 12:13).
7. He fills, anoints, or empowers (Eph. 5:18).
8. He guides into truth (Ps. 23:2; John 16:13; Acts 8:29; 10:19; 16 6–7; Rom. 8:14; Gal. 5:18).
9. He glorifies Christ (John 16:13–14).
10. He separates or calls for service (Acts 13:2).
11. He intercedes (Rom. 8:26).
12. He works (1 Cor. 12:11).
13. He speaks (1 Kings 22:24; Isa. 30:21; Luke 12:12; Acts 1:16; Gal. 4:6;).
14. He quickens (John 6:63).
15. He sanctifies (Rom. 15:16).
16. He was involved in the creation process (Gen. 1:2; Job 33:4; Ps. 104:30).

17. He is the inspiration of the scriptures (Acts 1:16; 28:25; 2 Tim. 3:16; 2 Peter 1:21).
18. He raised the dead (Rom. 8:11).
19. He gives ministering gifts (Rom. 12; 1 Cor. 12; Eph. 4).

Our desire as Christians should be to grow spiritually and allow our lives to be dominated by the Holy Spirit. Every believer has the indwelling of the Holy Spirit. However, not all are filled with the Holy Spirit. The indwelling of the Holy Spirit is a one-time occurrence, but the filling of the Holy Spirit happens many times throughout the believer's life.

The baptism, indwelling, and sanctification of the Holy Spirit are for all believers. The filling of the Holy Spirit is for Christian living and anointing for service. When we read of a person under the anointing, he or she is doing a service for God. The anointing of the Holy Spirit empowers an individual so the nonbeliever will be persuaded to come to Christ or so a believer will grow closer to Christ. As He wills, the Holy Spirit anoints an individual at a selected time to do a service; therefore, the anointing isn't on an individual for twenty-four hours a day, seven days a week. The only person who had the anointing without measure was Jesus. John 3:34 says, "For he whom God hath sent speaketh the words of God: for God giveth not the Spirit by measure unto him."

Jesus did all His miracles in accordance with the will of God. He was unlimited in the anointing. At Jesus's baptism, the Holy Spirit descended on Christ, lighting and illuminating Him. He was baptized not only in water but also in the Spirit. Matthew 3:16 says, "And Jesus, when he was baptized, went up straightway out of the water: and, lo, the heavens were opened unto him, and he saw the Spirit of God descending like a dove, and lighting upon him."

The lighting that came on Jesus was the Holy Spirit or the anointing. Though Jesus was anointed without measure, He wasn't exempt from trials and temptations of the devil. Soon after Jesus was baptized and anointed with the Spirit of God, He was tempted in the wilderness for forty days. What this suggests is that though God may permit His anointing to descend on us, it doesn't keep us from being tested and persecuted. The anointing on Jesus empowered Him to do the work His Father had sent Him to do.

After the devil tempted Jesus and Jesus began His ministry, He returned in the power and Spirit of God. He went about, preaching the gospel of the kingdom and healing the sick.

> And Jesus returned in the power of the Spirit into Galilee: and there went out a fame of him though all the region round about. (Luke 4:14)

> And Jesus went about all Galilee, teaching in their synagogues, and preaching the gospel of the kingdom, and healing all manner of sickness and all manner of disease among the people. (Matt. 4:23)

Peter preached to Cornelius and his family about how God anointed Jesus for His ministry (Acts 10:38).

Jesus ministered to the people as the Son of Man (a servant) and not as the Son of God. He was God in the flesh, but while He was in the flesh, He was subordinate to God the Father in respect to doing what God had sent Him to do. He did miracles to establish He was the Son of God and died on the cross to establish the foundation for salvation. Jesus was 100 percent God and 100 percent man. The human part of Jesus experienced anger, fatigue, and so forth in the physical nature; but the anointing on Jesus empowered Him for service. Philippians 2:7 says, "But [Jesus] made himself of no reputation, and took upon him the form of a servant, and was made in the likeness of men."

Jesus was anointed to operate in the following fivefold ministry offices:

1. Apostle: The word *apostle* in the Greek (*apostolos*) means "one sent forth."[2] God sent Jesus by the Holy Spirit. Hebrews 3:1 says, "Wherefore, holy brethren, partakers of the heavenly calling, consider the Apostle and High Priest of our profession, Christ Jesus."
2. Prophet: Jesus said, "Verily I say unto you, No prophet is accepted in his own country" (Luke 4:24). The woman at the well perceived Jesus to be a prophet (John 4:19).
3. Evangelist: Jesus went all over the land, preaching the kingdom of God. Luke 4:18 says, "The Spirit of the Lord is upon me, because he hath anointed me to preach the gospel to the poor."
4. Pastor: Jesus was proclaimed to be the Good Shepherd. The word *shepherd* is translated as "pastor." Jesus said, "I am the good shepherd" (John 10:14).
5. Teacher: Jesus did just as much teaching as preaching and healing. Matthew 9:35 says, "And Jesus went about all the cities and villages, teaching in their synagogues, and preaching the gospel of the kingdom, and healing every sickness and every disease among the people."

Every believer has the Holy Spirit dwelling on the inside, but the anointing is for serving others. The anointing will come on the believer to manifest a gift of the Holy Spirit or to serve in a particular fivefold ministry gift. The indwelling of the Holy Spirit is a blessing to those who are born again, but the anointing or the power of the Holy Spirit is given to be a blessing to others. Christ anoints individuals, but believers sometimes make the service about themselves rather than about Christ. Some even become so spiritual until they are untouchable. Consequently, they cannot

---

[2] Vine's Complete Expository Dictionary of Old and New Testament Words, © 1984, 1996, Thomas Nelson, Inc. Nashville, TN

identify with others. The anointing isn't on a believer all the time. Anyone under the anointing was in service for the Lord.

Matthew 28:19–20 says, "Go ye, therefore, and teach all nations, baptizing them in the name of the Father, and of the Son and of the Holy Spirit. Teaching them to observe all things whatsoever I have commanded you; and lo, I am with you always, even unto the end of the world."

The first calling on all believers is the great commission. All believers are to spread the gospel of Jesus Christ. In this effort, the believer should not only speak of the word but also live it. The believer cannot effectively tell the good news if he or she isn't living according to it. This is the primary calling on all believers. So many Christians profess a call on their lives. Moreover, they haven't yet acknowledged the high call of God. Sometimes God summons someone to repentance.

The apostle Paul addressed the Philippians about their behavior to live righteously before God and not to lean on self-righteousness. He made known his position to strive to know Christ in the power of His resurrection. Christ is the object of our faith. Paul strove for the prize of the upward calling of God. Philippians 3:14 says, "I press toward the mark for the prize of the high calling of God in Christ Jesus."

This isn't to say everyone has a calling to preach, but all Christians should be a witness for Christ. The believer should tell the unbeliever about Jesus Christ and how He changed his or her life. The witness is about what Jesus did for us and not what we have done for ourselves. When we are faithful to that call of God, He will anoint us for other service. None of us is perfect, but the idea is to strive to do our best to live for Christ.

Some of this may raise a question. Are the gifts of the Holy Spirit imperative for our day and time? The Holy Bible is more than just a historical book; it is a book of faith. If we limit the accounts to the early church fathers, then the gifts of the Holy

Spirit aren't applicable for our time. If we live by faith and the faith of the scriptures, then they are applicable for us today.

There are many who limit the establishment of the body of Christ to their local church or denomination. If those who limit the move and power of the Holy Spirit apply this standard to the establishment of a denomination, the gifts of the Holy Spirit wouldn't be for believers today. But the power of God isn't limited to the concepts of a denomination. The body of Christ or the church is growing daily. Since the body of Christ is a continuous growth of the kingdom of God, the empowerment of the Holy Spirit is for us today and will be until we reach the fullness of Christ. Ephesians 4:13 says, "Till we all come in the unity of the faith, and of the knowledge of the Son of God, unto a perfect man, unto the measure of the stature of the fulness of Christ."

The gifts of the Holy Spirit are a persuasive move of God to draw others to Him, believers and nonbelievers alike. The signs of faith don't come before a person believes, but signs will follow those who believe. Mark 16:17–18 says, "And these signs shall follow them that believe; In my name shall they cast out devils; they shall speak with new tongues; They shall take up serpents; and if they drink any deadly thing, it shall not hurt them; they shall lay hands on the sick, and they shall recover."

The anointing or power of the Holy Spirit will build the faith and encourage those who desire to do the ministry of God. It will induce those who lack faith in Christ to have more faith in Him. God is powerful, and He has put power in us (the Holy Spirit). This doesn't mean we are little gods, but what it does mean is that we are sons or daughters of God. The Holy Spirit will give the unction or urge to move at God's command. The ministry gifts are for the edifying of the church, the body of Christ. The gifts of the Holy Spirit are for the kingdom of God and the glorification of God. No individual can go into the ministry gifts just because he or she desires to do so.

Dr. Brian E. W. Cretter

The ministry gifts or fivefold ministry, as some call it, is for those God has called and sent to do a service for the church. These ministries are divinely appointed, and no one can appoint anyone to these offices. It is dangerous to serve in an office or ministry God hasn't appointed you to. If there is a ministry in your Spirit, the Lord will bring it out. God uses spiritually mature people to confirm the call He has put in your spirit. We shouldn't take it on ourselves to move without God's command. We must make sure the call is of God and not a thought of our own desires. We can desire a ministry for so long until it becomes part of us, and it becomes difficult to discern whether it is a call from God or our own desires. In so many cases, we limit the call of God to ministry preaching. There are many believers who are well versed in the word of God, but that doesn't necessarily mean they, male or female, have been called into the preaching ministry. In a general sense, every believer should be a proclaimer of the word of God so the unsaved may become saved.

> Go ye therefore, and teach all nations, baptizing them in the name of the Father, and of the Son, and of the Holy Ghost. (Matt. 28:19)

> And all things are of God, who hath reconciled us to himself and by Jesus Christ, and hath given us the Ministry of Reconciliation; to wit, that God was in Christ, reconciling the world unto himself, not imputing their trespasses unto them; and hath committed unto us the Word of reconciliation. (2 Cor. 5:18–19)

Many believe the order in which the apostle Paul gave the fivefold ministry or the ministry gifts is superior to one or the other. But the order in which the apostle Paul listed the ministry offices wasn't to establish superiority but to establish the order in which Christ gave them to the early church. All the ministry gifts should work together for the perfecting of the saints so the church will be edified and God will be glorified. Some people suggest that if the fivefold ministry isn't operating in the local church, the church won't reach its spiritual potential. The ministry gifts aren't limited to a denomination or a particular church. If the ministry gifts are received in the context of the body of Christ, the bride of Christ, the church, or the kingdom of God, they are in operation.

One must be anointed to receive one of these offices. Therefore, before believers can enter one of these offices, they first must be called and sent from God. Before the twelve disciples were called apostles, Jesus called them and prepared them before He sent them out. Upon the calling or receiving of any of these offices, one first must be called to preach or teach or do both. One who has been called to preach proclaims the gospel, and one who has been called to teach explains the word of God.

Although Paul was an apostle, his main ministry was to preach and teach to the Gentiles. Paul exercised his apostolic and prophetic offices out of his preaching ministry. So often we have ministers who build their ministries out of their apostolic or prophetic office rather than from their preaching or teaching ministry. This is a dangerous thing to do. Often it will lead to a spiritually bankrupt church. Jesus said, "Go ye into all the world, preach, and teach unto all nations" (Matt. 28:19; Mark 16:15). He didn't say, "Go ye into all the world with a prophetic message and laying on of hands." The great commission is to preach or teach the word of God, to draw the unsaved and teach them to be disciples of Christ.

When God calls people to preach or teach His word, they must first be faithful to that ministry. Faithfulness is the key. You must be faithful, and your preaching or teaching ministry must be proved. Many people claim they have been called to preach, but they aren't faithful. They don't want to be tried by the fires of life to serve as messengers of God. There must be much sacrificing, studying, and praying to rightly divide the word of God. A proved and faithful ministry will speak for itself.

NOTES

CHAPTER 2
The Weapons of Warfare

For though we walk in the flesh, we do not war after the flesh: (For the weapons of our warfare are not carnal, but mighty through God to the pulling down of strongholds).
—2 Corinthians 10:3–4

The weapons of our warfare aren't carnal but spiritual. God has given us spiritual weapons from heaven. The apostle Paul recognized he was human and wasn't exempt from the infirmities of life's trials. Though the apostle was one of the most gifted men in the biblical recordings, he didn't act as though he were super spiritual, exempt from the attacks of the enemy.

Some Christians believe that just because God anointed them with a certain gift, they are exempt from the attacks of the devil and the trials of this world. That idea is far from the truth. After Jesus's baptism in the Jordan River, the Spirit led Him into the wilderness to be tempted by the devil. Anyone who is striving to do the will of God will be tested and tried. No one is exempt from infirmities and human corruption. The apostle Paul realized his strength isn't in himself but in God and His power. Paul was a learned man and didn't totally rely on human fallible intellect.

The carnal weapons of human ingenuity, organizing ability, powerful propaganda, charm, or personality are ineffectual in the ceaseless act of pulling down the strongholds bound up by evil. The carnal weapons may win the battle temporarily, but eventually the fortress of evil will have to be torn down. This warfare is a spiritual one. Therefore, our weapons must be those of the Spirit. We will fight a losing battle if we try to fight evil in our own strength. Zechariah 4:6 says, "Not by might, nor by power, but by my Spirit, saith the Lord of Host."

The apostle Paul's strength and courage lay in the permanent and unfailing Spirit of God. He was a man in Christ and empowered by the Holy Spirit. The Lord, our God, bestows a gift or gifts to us. It isn't our will, but it is the Spirit of the Lord who gives as He wills. He is the source of our strength and empowerment. Jesus came as a man—and not only as God; He came as a servant. The Holy Spirit anointed Him to do the will of His Father. The gifts of the Spirit manifested throughout the ministry of Jesus Christ. The power of God is invincible. He has given the gifts of the Holy Spirit to the body of Christ as the weapons of our warfare.

The war we are in is an invisible war going on in the spirit realm. Often the results of a battle will manifest in the natural realm. How do we recognize the opposition? How do we fight this battle? Many believers are in a warfare and don't know it. Some recognize the enemy but don't know how to fight the battle and be victorious.

The main weapon of our warfare is the Holy Spirit, who seals us. He indwells us and empowers us for service. The Holy Spirit brings to our remembrance what we have studied. He is our Comforter who guides us into all truth. What the Holy Spirit hears and says comes from Christ. John 16:13 says, "Howbeit, when he, the Spirit of truth is come, he will guide you into all truth: for he shall not speak of himself; but whatsoever he shall hear, that shall he speak; and he will show you things to come."

The Holy Spirit empowers us for His service. Without His anointing in our lives, we can do nothing. Many are doing a service but not according to the guidance of the Holy Spirit. In our modern times, people are teaching and preaching without power. The Spirit of God will empower as He wills and not as we will. There is a thirst or hunger for the gifts of the Holy Spirit. The zeal of some people is energized in the wrong direction. So many believers seek the gifts of the Holy Spirit for prestige.

We must remember that the anointing is the empowerment of the Spirit of the Anointed One. Some people are more anointed than others because of the tasks God has given them. Some believers yield themselves to the workings of the Holy Spirit at different stages. Some may submit more than others. The more believers submit to the Holy Spirit, the more the Holy Spirit will use them. Acts 1:8 says, "But ye shall receive power, after that the Holy Ghost is come upon you: and ye shall be witnesses unto me both in Jerusalem, and in all Judaea, and in Samaria, and unto the uttermost part of the earth."

Jesus commanded His disciples to go to Jerusalem and wait for the power of the Holy Spirit. This power had to come on them before they could go out and be a witness for Christ. The Greek word here for "power" is *dunamis*. *Dunamis* is defined "to strengthen, have ability or miraculous power[3]." The Holy Spirit gives us help and aids us for the work of kingdom building. We believers cannot afford to be in this warfare without the power of the Holy Spirit. The Holy Spirit will empower us for the task Jesus Christ commanded us to do in Mark 16:17–18. "And these signs shall follow them that believe; In my name shall they cast out devils; they shall speak with new tongues; They shall take up serpents; and if they drink any deadly thing, it shall not hurt them; they shall lay hands on the sick, and they shall recover."

For the Holy Spirit to use us effectively, we must prepare ourselves daily. We do this, first, by reading and meditating on the word of God; and, second, by having a productive prayer life.

---

[3] Vine's expository dictionary of new testament word, unbridged edition, MacDonald Publishing Company Mclean, VA, 22101

These disciplines will strength our inner man. When the disciples went to Jerusalem for the Passover, they were in one accord in prayer. Because of their obedience to Christ and sincerity in prayer, the Spirit of the Lord came on them and gave them power. Acts 2:2–4 says, "And suddenly there came a sound from heaven as of a rushing mighty wind, and it filled all the house where they were sitting. And there appeared unto them cloven tongues like as of fire, and it sat upon each of them. And they were all filled with the Holy Ghost, and began to speak with other tongues, as the Spirit gave them utterance."

The disciples could speak with other tongues as the Spirit gave them power to do so. Many believers project a gift of the Holy Spirit with their wills rather than with the will of the Holy Spirit.

Another weapon of our warfare is the word of God. The Holy Bible identifies the enemy and how he operates. It is a book of faith. We must believe the word of God and take God at His word. His word is the sword the apostle Paul talked about in Roman 1:16. Our confidence in the word of God should be from Genesis to Revelation. Some Christians try to explain away the scriptures by keeping them in their historical context. Some people believe only parts of the Bible. God's word is very much as applicable in our modern times as it was in biblical history. Jesus said, "Verily, verily, I say unto you, He that believeth on me, the works that I do shall he do also; and greater works than these shall he do; because I go unto my Father" (John 14:12). If Jesus said it, we should believe it.

We must read and meditate on God's word. When God's word is in our hearts and spirits, God the Holy Spirit will give us a word for the time of warfare. The Comforter will bring the scriptures, what we have stored in our hearts, back to our remembrance. He will give us the word for the occasion at hand. God reminds us of His written word by leading us in the Logos or by a *rhema*. The Logos is the Holy Writ in its entirety. A *rhema* word is a portion of scripture or scriptures abstracted from the Logos for a specific time and purpose.

Both Ephesians 6:17 and Romans 10:17 speak of the *rhema* word of God. Ephesians 6:17, for example, gives a *rhema* word for spiritual warfare. "And take the helmet of salvation, and the sword of the Spirit, which is the word of God."

The apostle Paul taught us in Ephesians 6 about putting on the whole armor of God. The armor of God equips and protects us for the warfare. Paul used the sword as the word of God. The whole armor is for protection; the two-edge sword is the only offensive weapon that cuts back and forth and penetrates deeply. It is the word of God and the power of the Holy Spirit that pull down strongholds. When the enemy has us under attack, the Lord will bring forth a *rhema* word to combat Satan and his angels.

Romans 10:17 speaks a *rhema* word as a word of faith. We must have faith to fight this battle (Rom. 10:17). "So, then faith cometh by hearing, and hearing by the word of God." The *rhema* word here comes by hearing the word of God. By hearing the word, we can increase our faith as well. By the preached word, we may hear and receive. A person anointed to preach the word of God would infiltrate our hearts. The word of God will give us not only saving faith but also faith in other areas of our lives. Faith is of essence to have the gifts of the Holy Spirit. If you don't believe, you won't receive.

> Now there are diversities of gifts, but the same Spirit. And there are differences of administrations, but the same Lord. And there are diversities of operations, but it is the same God which worketh all in all. But the manifestation of the Spirit is given to every man to profit withal. For to one is given by the Spirit the word of wisdom; to another the word of knowledge by the same Spirit; To another faith by the same Spirit; to another the gifts of healing by the same Spirit; To another the working of miracles; to another prophecy; to

> another discerning of spirits; to another divers
> kinds of tongues; to another the interpretation of
> tongues: But all these worketh that one and the
> selfsame Spirit, dividing to every man severally as
> he will. (1 Cor. 12:4–11)

The Holy Spirit gives all nine gifts the apostle Paul listed. These gifts are for every person in the body of Christ. There is competition in the body of Christ, for instance, such as with the church in Corinth; some think their gift is better than the next person's gift. All gifts are for the work of the ministry and kingdom building. Some modern churches are dogmatic about their denominational doctrine. The gifts of the Holy Spirit isn't just for a particular denomination, but is for the purpose of glorifying God, edifying the church, and evangelizing the world. These gifts of the Holy Spirit are divided in three sections: revelation gifts, power gifts, and vocal gifts.

CHAPTER 3
The Gifts of the Holy Spirit

Now concerning spiritual gifts, brethren,
I would not have you ignorant.

1Corinthians 12:1

There are two foundations in scripture for the gifts of the Holy Spirit to operate effectively in the church body: unity and love. Throughout the Pauline Epistles, the apostle Paul stressed unity in the body of Christ. In our modern times, we have many denominations. I believe God allowed several denominations because not everybody will receive the plan of salvation in the same way. The devil, however, has taken the concept of denominationalism and caused division in the body of Christ. He planted the idea that one denomination is better than another. If a denomination preaches and teaches that Jesus Christ is the Messiah and Savior of the world, then we all are brothers and sisters in Christ.

Some denominations have the label of being traditional. A denomination defines its own traditions. The denomination you belong to defines your traditions. Many people must separate what is tradition from what is biblical. Some things that go on in the local church are scriptural rather than traditional.

God is calling for unity in the body of Christ. Unity in the body of Christ increases its strength and power for this daily spiritual warfare we encounter in these last days. It is necessary that different ministries support one another for the cause of Jesus Christ. The body of Christ is beginning to unify. Believers in the body of Christ are coming together to spread the gospel of Jesus Christ and do the work of the ministry despite their denomination. God is raising up leaders who are concerned about ministry and kingdom building.

For the church to be effective to the utmost, we must let the head of the church be the head and try to have unity in the local church body. Some churches or denominations have their own agenda, but they aren't on God's agenda. We shouldn't judge one another or have any cliques in the church. In its beginning stages, the church had leaders who were of one accord and in one place for prayer and supplication. When they were with one accord, there came a sound from heaven as a rushing, mighty wind, and cloven tongues like as of fire touched each of them. Then they were filled with the Holy Spirit.

> These all continued with one accord in prayer and supplication, with the women, and Mary the mother of Jesus, and with his brethren. (Acts 1:14)

> And when the day of Pentecost was fully come, they were all with one accord in one place. And suddenly there came a sound from heaven as of a rushing mighty wind, and it filled all the house where they were sitting. And there appeared unto them cloven tongues like as of fire, and it sat upon each of them. (Acts 2:1–3)

Though there are many denominations in the body of Christ, we must function out of love, going beyond our denominational doctrines, our differences, and come together as though there are no denominations. The blood of Jesus Christ binds us together and redeems us; His Holy Spirit regenerates us. We are all brothers and sisters in Christ Jesus. No matter what denomination you are part of—if we are born again in Christ Jesus, we are of one body, the body of Christ. First Corinthians 12:13 says, "For as the body is one, and hath many members, and all the members of that one body, being many, are one body: so also is Christ. For by one Spirit are we all baptized into one body, whether we be bond or free; and have been all made to drink into one Spirit."

If one is contrary to unity in the body of Christ, the gifts of the Holy Spirit won't operate in his or her life. The gifts of the Holy Spirit are intended for edifying the church. God's power is manifested through the gifts of the Holy Spirit. We can desire different gifts, but the Holy Spirit gives spiritual gifts as He wills. God wants us to flow or commune in the body of Christ. The gifts of the Holy Spirit won't operate effectively when we become selfish and isolate ourselves from the rest of the church.

So many Christians define their spiritual growth by the gifts of the Holy Spirit. These aren't an indication of one's spiritual growth, but they do show the manifestation of the fruit of the Holy Spirit and a changed life. In Acts 19:1–6, the apostle Paul went to Ephesus and found twelve of John the Baptist's disciples. John the Baptist baptized unto repentance but not unto salvation in Christ Jesus. Paul asked them whether they had received the Holy Spirit. The twelve hadn't even heard of the Holy Spirit. Therefore, Paul explained to them that they had to believe in Jesus Christ. When they heard this, they believed. Paul baptized them in the name of Jesus Christ, then laid hands on them; they received the Holy Spirit and began to speak with tongues and prophesied. Does this mean they reached spiritual maturity right then? Spiritual maturity comes over time as maturity does in the natural realm.

There is another account in Acts 8:14–17. Many in the church blame church leaders for their lack of spiritual growth. It isn't always the leader but the one who sits in the pew who is at fault. In Acts 8:6, Luke recorded, "The people with one accord gave heed unto those things which Philip spake, hearing and seeing the miracles which he did." Ask yourself, am I lacking spiritual growth because of the leader or because I'm not hearing or seeing? Romans 10:17, says, "So then faith come by hearing and hearing by the word of God." Some entertain the thoughts, *I am really great* and *I am really anointed.* It isn't our greatness or anointing, but God is great, and His Spirit does the anointing. The gifts of the Holy Spirit are intended for service to others. We are who we are because of the grace of God. For one to receive these mighty gifts of God, one must have a genuine love for His people.

The gifts are good, but they are mostly effective when ministered in love. The apostle Paul said, "But covet earnestly the best gifts; and yet show I unto you a more excellent way" (1 Cor. 12:31; compare to 1 Cor. 13).

Love is the second foundation for the church and the world. It was through God's love that He gave His only begotten Son for the world. It is through God's love that He has sustained the world. God's love should radiate through the entire body of Christ. It is through the show of love that God draws others into His kingdom. There should be a thrust of love in and through the body of Christ. John 13:34–35 says, "A new commandment I give unto you, That ye love one another; as I have loved you, that ye also love one another. By this shall all men know that ye are my disciples, if ye have love one to another."

Did Jesus say, "By the gifts of the Comforter men will know you are my disciples"? Did Jesus say, "When you speak in an unknown tongue or prophecy, men will know you are my disciples"? He said, "If you love one another men shall know you are disciples" Joh. 13:35. Love is the main ingredient. God is love.

The Greek word for God's love is *agape.* Agape love or God's love is unconditional love. Unconditional love is the love that looks beyond a person's faults. Agape looks to help those who are less fortunate. God's love isn't based on how we may feel. If the love of God were based on feelings, Christians would judge even the slightest little thing. There are many carnal-minded Christians who are judging others because they feel like either they are better than the others or the others just aren't worthy. God's expectations of us all are to live His standards and not our own standards or the standards of others. If we measure ourselves according to the word of God, there will be less judgment and more mercy.

In 1 Corinthians 13, the apostle Paul taught the church about love. He said, "Though I speak with the tongues of men and of angels, and haven't charity, I am become as sounding brass, or a tinkling cymbal"1 Co. 13:1. He listed his spiritual gift and the works of his ministry and concluded that if he didn't have love, it profited him nothing, and he was nothing. He went on to give the characteristics of this unconditional love. In his epilogue, he gave the concept that no one knows it all and gave love superiority over hope and faith. The love of God causes the church to operate effectively and with the right motives.

The Corinthians operated in the gifts of the Holy Spirit, but they were a carnal- minded church. The church was well established, but they were babes in Christ. Those who are spiritually immature will cause division, envy, and strife in the church. First Corinthians 3:1–3 says, "And I, brethren, could not speak unto you as unto spiritual, but as unto carnal, even as unto babes in Christ. I have fed you with milk, and not with meat: for hitherto ye were not able to bear it, neither ye now are ye able. For ye are yet carnal: for whereas there is among you envying, and strife, and divisions, are ye not carnal, and walk as men?"

How great the anointing, the power, the glory of God would be if the church or the body of Christ showed forth the love of God. The power of God will come forth more effectively through the gifts of the Holy Spirit. The healing of the sick will manifest. Signs, wonders, and the working of miracles will show. The speaking in an unknown tongue with the interpretation will edify the church, and the unbeliever will believe.

Love is the most majestic way to show we are the disciples of Christ. God's power will manifest through those who genuinely love Him and His people.

NOTES

CHAPTER 4
The Revelation Gifts

---◇---

For to one is given by the Spirit word of wisdom; to another the word of knowledge by the same Spirit; to another discerning of spirits. 1 Corinthians 12:8…10

These gifts have to do with information revealed to a person supernaturally. The person hasn't conceived, heard, or seen the revelation in the natural realm. The information revealed is outside natural reasoning and logic. Revelation gifts come by a direct word from God, dreams, or visions. The revelation gifts give spiritual insight to hidden things. Upon the revelation gifts, the use of the other gifts will be demonstrated appropriately.

The Word of Wisdom

The Holy Bible speaks of different kinds of wisdom. We have God's wisdom, natural wisdom, and devilish wisdom. Natural wisdom is earthly wisdom. One learns wisdom through trial and error. The wisdom we learn on earth is by cause and effect. The apostle James talked about this wisdom in James 3:13. The gift of the word of wisdom goes beyond what we rely on as common sense or natural understanding. In contrast to man's wisdom, the word of wisdom is a portion of God's wisdom. The word of wisdom comes through the power of the Holy Spirit, who indwells us.

This wisdom gives events that will happen in the future. The word of wisdom is supernaturally revealed for a divine purpose. God doesn't reveal the whole condition but gives only a segment of His omniscience. The wisdom of God revealed always points to the event happening on earth. The word of wisdom can come to an individual for another individual or to a church collectively. When the Holy Spirit gives a revelation as such, that doesn't mean a person is a know-it-all. The revelation isn't based on a person's intellectual knowledge. God gives people wisdom for a situation at a particular time. Sometimes the fulfillment isn't in the immediate future but can be days, months, or years away.

The Old Testament prophets all had the word of wisdom and could tell what was to come. These were men like Daniel, Noah, Ezekiel, Isaiah, and David; and there are others. The Holy Spirit led them then like the Holy Spirit leads us now. Isaiah 54:17 is a word of wisdom given to the prophet Isaiah, one we often use these days. "No weapon that is formed against thee shall prosper; and every tongue that shall rise against thee in judgment thou shalt condemn. This is the heritage of the servants of the Lord, and their righteousness is of me, saith the Lord."

This word of wisdom was given to Isaiah to give to the children of Israel prior to their seventy years of captivity. The word of wisdom is a word of hope, warning, encouragement, and faith. The Lord gave the apostle Paul a word of wisdom. Act 23:11 says, "And the night following the Lord stood by him, and said, Be of good cheer, Paul: for as thou hast testified of me in Jerusalem, so must thou bear witness also at Rome."

Paul stood before a council made up of Pharisees and Sadducees. They vowed to kill Paul for the spreading of the gospel of Jesus Christ. More than forty men conspired against Paul. These men were desperate to the point that they wouldn't eat or drink anything until they had killed the apostle. The apostle's life was in danger.

The Lord gave Paul a word of encouragement as well as a word of wisdom. He was thrown in prison, with his life threatened, but he knew he wasn't going to die because of the word of wisdom the Lord had given him. The apostle Paul wouldn't have known he was going to preach in Rome except by the word of wisdom given to him.

The word of wisdom demonstrates to us what is going on now or in the future. It will reveal those things we cannot see, the mysteries of life. We must remember that the word of wisdom, like all the gifts, should be understood in the spiritual realm. God communicates with us in our inner man. Carnal-minded believers or those in the world won't understand it. The word given will sound like foolishness. We should have faith and be sensitive to the voice of the Holy Spirit in our lives.   First Corinthians 2:13–14 says, "Which things also we speak, not in the words which man's wisdom teacheth, but which the Holy Ghost teacheth; comparing spiritual things with spiritual. But the natural man receiveth not the things of the Spirit of God: for they are foolishness unto him: neither can he know them, because they are spiritually discerned."

The gift of the word of wisdom is very important in our lives today. It will keep us from making a lot of mistakes. We used to say in the past, "If I knew then what I know now, I wouldn't have done it." The word of wisdom will show us things to come so we won't have to make that statement too often.

The Word of Knowledge

The word of knowledge deals with facts. It reveals things of the past or the present. It will show us things in the here and now. The word of knowledge reveals facts that are hidden; rather it is about an individual, nation, or church. It is a fact shown that wasn't known in any form in the natural realm. It is a supernatural revelation from God to the believer. A word of knowledge can be one word, sentence, or paragraph. The recipient of the word must know it is God and trust Him.

Dr. Brian E. W. Cretter

God sends us a word of knowledge for many reasons. He will send a word of warning and encouragement. Often when we should make decisions, the Holy Spirit will quicken our spirits with a word of knowledge. We must be sensitive to the Holy Spirit. Sometimes the word of knowledge will come in seconds. It may be repeated, but we must catch the word, sentence, or phrase when it comes.

In Acts 10, the Lord sent a word of knowledge to a man named Cornelius. Cornelius believed God, but he wasn't saved. While he was in prayer, a word of knowledge came to him. The Lord told him to send three men to Joppa. There was a man there by the name of Simon. Acts 10:4–5 says, "And when he (Cornelius) looked on him, he was afraid, and said, What is it, Lord? And he said unto him, Thy prayers and thine alms are come up for a memorial before God. And now send men to Joppa, and call for one Simon, whose surname is Peter."

The Lord came to apostle Peter in a vision concerning Peter's judging of others, the Gentiles. While Peter thought on the vision, a word of knowledge came to him. Acts 10:19–21 says, "While Peter thought on the vision, the Spirit said unto him, Behold, three men seek thee. Arise therefore, and get thee down, and go with them, doubting nothing: for I have sent them. Then Peter went down to the men which were sent unto him from Cornelius; and said, Behold, I am he whom ye seek: what is the cause wherefore ye are come?"

While Peter was thinking and praying, he had no idea men had been sent from Cornelius. The Spirit of the Lord spoke to Peter and said there were three men seeking him. Because of the Cornelius devotion and the word of knowledge that came to Cornelius and Peter, salvation came to Cornelius and his whole house.

In the Old Testament, Elijah received a word of knowledge from God. Elijah was discouraged and feared for his life. "And he said, I have been very jealous for the Lord God of hosts: because the children of Israel have forsaken thy covenant, thrown down thine altars, and slain thy prophets with the sword; and I, even I only, am left; and they seek my life, to take it away ... Yet I have left me seven thousand in Israel, all the knees which have not bowed unto Baal, and every mouth which hath not kissed him" (1 Kings 19:14, 18).

The prophet Elijah had defeated the prophet of Baal, but there was a woman named Jezebel who threatened to kill him. Elijah left the city, went to Beer-Sheba, and sat under a juniper tree. Elijah thought he was the only one of God's prophets. The Lord gave Elijah instructions and duties. In conjunction with the newly appointed task, God gave Elijah a word of knowledge. There were seven thousand prophets of God who had neither bowed to Baal nor kissed the idol. Then He said to go and anoint Elisha as a prophet and Jehu as king.

When the Holy Spirit gives us a word of knowledge, it causes immediate action. The word of knowledge works hand in hand with healings. If someone has a terminal illness, the Lord will give the name of that illness so the recipient may be healed. Sometimes the word of knowledge will reveal sin in a person's life. Some sicknesses are the result of sin. Jesus Christ often had to forgive people of their sin so they could receive their healing.

We must believe by faith the word the Lord has given us. If we are to help others, the gift of the word of knowledge is for all who believe.

Discerning of Spirits

There are different spirits operating in the world. We have the Holy Spirit, the devil spirit, and the human spirit. In our modern times, we must have the discerning of spirit. There are different spirits in operation daily. Twenty-four hours a day, there is angelic warfare going on. God wants us to know His Spirit as well as the devil spirit. How can we engage in warfare or discern spirits if we don't recognize Satan's spirits? First Corinthians 14:10 says, "There are, it may be, so many kinds of voices in the world, and none of them is without signification."

I have heard people say, "I have the gift of discernment." There is no such gift in the Bible. There are many spirits in operation during the worship experience. Not every spirit that speaks is the Holy Spirit. Not every thought that enters your mind is of the Holy Spirit. Not everybody who comes to you and says, "Thus saith the Lord" is of God. We must know the difference. John 10:27 says, "My sheep hear my voice, and I know them, and they follow me."

There are many people who project they have arrived. When they get to that point, they will listen to every voice and are ripe for the devil to send spiritual deception their way. Satan can come as an angel of light. This means in the light not only of a minister but also of a layperson. Too many people claim a heavy anointing when, in contrast, they aren't as anointed as they claim to be.

The voice of the Holy Spirit comes from within, whereas all other voices come from outside through the ear. Neither a person's speech nor his or her actions is a signal that he or she is of God. There are people in church who shout with praises, speak in tongues, and even dance when the music starts to play. Does that mean they are under the unction of the Holy Spirit?

The gift of discerning of spirits isn't given based on outward appearance or suspicion. Often people say they have discerned a spirit based on what they have heard. The discerning of spirit has nothing to do with what we see in the natural realm or think. It has everything to do with what God allows us to see in the spiritual realm.

In the gift of discerning of spirit, God allows a believer to see into the spirit world. Behind every action there is a motive, and behind every motive there is a spirit. The Holy Spirit will give us the unction if it is a good spirit or a bad spirit.

We profess to know God. We must know the spirit of our adversary as well. The Holy Spirit will let us know the difference between truth and mistake. The Holy Spirit will reveal what induces a person to do good or bad. He won't show us everything about a person. He will show the spirit for that particular moment and purpose.

The apostle Paul recognized a deceiving spirit, but he didn't recognize it right away. It was days before the Lord revealed the spirit to him. Acts 16:16–18 says, "And it came to pass, as we went to prayer, a certain damsel possessed with a spirit of divination met us, which brought her masters much gain by soothsaying: The same followed Paul and us, and cried, saying, These men are the servants of the most high God, which show unto us the way of salvation. And this did she many days. But Paul, being grieved, turned and said to the spirit, I command thee in the name of Jesus Christ to come out of her. And he came out the same hour."

The apostle Paul and others were on their way to prayer. The young lady had a spirit of divination; in other words, she practiced fortune-telling. This is something the woman did in her personal life. She made a lot of money doing it for a living. This woman followed them and said all the right things. Who would have thought this woman had a python spirit and was a worshipper of Apollo?

Many people in the church practice black magic and witchcraft. It will take God to reveal these spirits by the gift of the discerning of spirits. If the Holy Spirit doesn't reveal the spirit, we can be deceived. Not only will the Holy Spirit show what kind of spirit, but He will also show the motive of the spirit. Any spirit and motive outside the Holy Spirit seek to kill, steal, and destroy.

How did Paul discern the woman was possessed with an evil spirit? She followed them for days. She said religious things. Everything sounded and looked good. The Lord had to show the apostle Paul through the gift of discerning of spirits. Acts 16:18 says, "But Paul, being grieved, turned and said to the spirit, I command thee in the name of Jesus Christ to come out of her."

This is how the Lord shows us there is a spirit of error. Our spirits will be grieved. Somehow, we will feel this isn't right deep inside our inner man. Our spirits will be restless. We must witness to and/or cast that spirit out of the person in Jesus's name. The devil cannot possess those who are babes in church, but they can be *obsessed*. They are under the influence of the spirit of the adversary.

There was a time at my church when we were gathered around the altar for prayer. As one of the ministers was praying, a woman there had a whining spirit. She said, "Hallelujah" in a whining way. She was disruptive to those around. My spirit became grieved. I said in a low voice, "Silence in the name of Jesus." Immediately the whining stopped.

Be not deceived; the devil is doing more to rage war on the saints of God. In our modern time, he disguises himself and his spirits in the form of religion. There are many people saying and doing things in the name of Jesus. There are people in the church practicing voodoo, witchcraft, and all kinds of wickedness.

The discerning of spirit works with the word of knowledge. Not only will the Holy Spirit show us a spirit, but He will also show what kind of spirit it is.

One day a lady was teaching Sunday school. She made a statement about doing something in faith. She said, "While your husband is sleep, you are to pray and speak faith over him." As I sat there, my spirit was troubled. The Lord told me that was a selfish spirit and a spirit of witchcraft.

The gift of discerning of spirits allows a person to see what others cannot. The more you learn about God's word and the increased desire for the gift of discerning of spirits, the Holy Spirit will manifest it as He wills. Be prepared. The devil gets mad at you for desiring this weapon of warfare. This weapon recognizes and exposes Satan and his angels.

CHAPTER 5
The Power Gifts

———◇———

To another faith by the same Spirit; to another the gifts of
healing by the same Spirit; To another the working of miracles.
—1 Corinthians 12:9–10

Often these gifts of the Holy Spirit are called "sign gifts." These
are manifested in the natural realm. People today desire these
gifts more than the others, because they bring prestige. If people
desire these gifts for gain and prestige, they are headed for a big
disappointment. In many cases, people pretend they have these
gifts. They will lay hands on the sick but have no results. The Bible
teaches that we shouldn't quickly lay hands on people. Pretending
to have an anointing you don't have is dangerous. It hinders the
faith of those who sincerely desire to be healed, and it can damage
the soul of the believer.

The Gift of Faith

There are many kinds of faith. Everybody has natural faith. When
you go to work on Monday, you have the faith that your employer
will pay you on Friday. When farmers sow seeds in the ground,
they believe the seeds will bring about a harvest. Natural faith has
nothing to do with the supernatural gift of faith.

Then there is saving faith. Often people confuse saving faith with having the gift of faith. Saving faith is when people hear the gospel preached; they will be saved and have eternal life with Jesus Christ. Every born-again believer has saving faith. Saving faith is needed not only for eternal life but also for healing. People can become ill, pray a prayer, quote a scripture, and believe God for their healing.

Hebrews 11:1 says, "Now faith is the substance of things hoped for, the evidence of things not seen." This faith in the book of Hebrews talks about regular faith. This faith is the standard for hope. We hope for the substance of whatever that may be, and we have the faith that it will happen.

The gift of faith is the achievement of something without human effort or explanation. It achieves the impossible. It is when God moves through the power of the Holy Spirit on the behavior of the believer. The impossible isn't attained in the ordinary sense but done in a way that the only explanation is God being supernaturally moved. The gift of faith is the power of the Holy Spirit working through and in us. This area of faith often works in divine protection and provision. It functions in the area where there is nothing we can do, and we have done all we could do. Jesus illustrated the gift of faith on the Sea of Galilee.

Mark 4:39 says, "And he arose, and rebuked the wind, and said unto the sea, Peace, be still. And the wind ceased, and there was a great calm." Jesus and His disciple were in a storm, and the waves started to fill the ship. The disciples did all they knew how to do. They couldn't do anything to save themselves. They woke Jesus, who was asleep on the ship. Jesus stood on the deck of the ship and spoke a word of faith: "Peace, be still." The storm immediately ceased.

The gift of faith is unlimited. It has no limitations because God is the source. When we have the power of God working through us, we become more than conquerors. A conqueror defeats one who is of equal strength. To be more than a conqueror is to defeat one or a situation that is greater than you.

Roman 8:37, "Nay, in all these things we are more than conquerors through him that loved us." We are more than conquerors only through God who loves us. God does the conquering. He is the one who will fight your battles. As God, through the power of the Holy Spirit, opens the door, we rejoice because we know it has nothing to do with human effort but everything to do with divine intervention.

Daniel had the gift of faith. In Daniel 6, when he was about to be put in the lions' den, he had faith that God wasn't going to let the lions have him for dinner. The men put him in the lions' den, but by the next morning, Daniel hadn't suffered any hurt.

The three Hebrew boys who faced a fiery furnace had the gift of faith. Nebuchadnezzar heated the furnace seven time its original heat. The Hebrew boys refused to bow down to the image Nebuchadnezzar had built. While they were in the furnace, God rescued them, and no harm was done to them. The gift of faith gives us the kind of faith in which we totally depend on God and His power.

The Holy Spirit gives us the gift of faith because God wants to do something to help or bless somebody. God can use the gift of faith to stop some evil workings in your life or the lives of others. The Lord gives us power for only what the situation calls for. We must read the word of God to get it down in our hearts and spirits. The Holy Spirit will bring to our remembrance scriptures related to the gift of faith or power scriptures.

The Gift of Healings

The gifts of healing are the only gifts of the nine gifts written in the plural form. This suggests that there are different operations of this gift. There are all kinds of sicknesses and diseases. Some sickness can be caused by an accident, some by spirit of infirmity or even by satanic oppression. What are the gifts of healing? They are the virtue or power of God flowing through an individual to drive out affliction in Jesus's name. They are given as the Spirit wills.

There is no set way for these gifts to operate. The Lord may tell you just to speak a word of healing. He might lead you to lay hands on someone or to tell someone to read a scripture and believe.

This gift can operate with the word of knowledge. It would take the word of knowledge to reveal the hidden disease a person might have. The Holy Spirit will reveal a certain kind of disease for a person to call out, and that person gets healed. These gifts of healing will work on behalf of an unbeliever. For the unbeliever, it is most important to get saved, but an unbeliever can be healed without being saved.

No one person can heal all diseases or sickness. If one person could heal all manner of diseases, he or she would be like God. When people feel they are God in a sense, pride steps in and ultimately becomes a dangerous disposition. Lucifer was cast out of heaven because of pride and his desire to be like God.

Jesus Christ is the only person able to heal all manner of diseases. The gifts of healing cause one to move according to the sickness. Not all healings are done the same way. Jesus healed people according to their illness. He recognized the condition and healing accordingly.

For the man who was blind from birth, Jesus spat on the ground and made clay. He anointed the man's eye and told him to go wash in the pool of Siloam.

Blind Bartimaeus sat by the road, begging. He heard Jesus was coming his way and cried out to Him. Jesus told the crowd to bring him here. Jesus asked him, "What wilt thou that I should do unto thee?" Bartimaeus answered him, "Lord, that I might receive my sight." Jesus said to him, "Go thy way; thy faith hath made thee whole" Mar. 10: 51-52.

A man brought his son for the disciples to heal. The son was a lunatic, and the disciples couldn't heal him. Jesus and three of His disciples came down from the mountain. Jesus saw the boy's condition and healed him by saying, "Thou dumb and deaf spirit, I charge thee, come out of him, and enter no more into him." Jesus healed these three cases in different ways.

The gifts of healing have their limits and are limited by unbelief. The person God wants to use must have faith, and the recipient must have faith in God. Unbelief can hinder one's healing. Another point of limitations is that the person with the gift of healing must operate in the area in which the Holy Spirit called him or her. People have the gifts of healing in different areas. One ministry can have the anointing to heal in one area while another ministry can have the anointing to heal in another one.

Through this ministry the Lord endows one with this gift to pray specifically for diseases.

The Gift of Working Miracles

The working of miracles comes from the power of God working through you. It is an act of God speaking and causing something to come to pass. It is a supernatural occurrence that goes beyond our natural comprehension. The Greek word for "work" is *energema*. It is the word in which we get our English word *energy*. The Greek word for *miracle* is *dunamis*. This is the root word for our English word *dynamite*. The working of miracles is God's supernatural intervention in the normal course of nature. This gift calls for action. God entrusts His energy and powers to the believer. Having this gift, we participate in the process.

The power of God can flow through our hands or any part of our bodies. Though God uses our bodies as instruments, the healing is totally from the strength of God. He works the miracle in ways and strength we don't normally have. It is the virtue of the Spirit of God working through us to do something that's not natural or normal. For the gift of working miracles, the Holy Spirit gives creative powers as He wills. The Lord God can use people and animals.

Balak, the king of the Moabites, wanted Balaam to curse the children of Israel so he could defeat them. But Balaam, the prophet of God, wouldn't take the bribes of the Moabite king. The Lord spoke to Balaam and told him not to go with the Moabites. When the morning came, the Moabites came to Balaam. He saddled his donkey and went with them. This action of Balaam angered the Lord (Num. 22:21–30).

The Lord sent an angel to appear in the path of the donkey three times. The donkey refused to go in the direction of the angel. Balaam hit the donkey each time. Then God used the mouth of the donkey. Numbers 22:28–30 says, "And the Lord opened the mouth of the ass, and she said unto Balaam, What have I done unto thee, that thou hast smitten me these three times? And Balaam said unto the ass, Because thou hast mocked me: I would there were a sword in mine hand, for now would I kill thee. And the ass said unto Balaam, Am not I thine ass, upon which thou hast ridden ever since I was thine unto this day? was I ever wont to do so unto thee? And he said, Nay."

This miracle is abnormal to our reasoning. God used the vocal cords of the donkey, and Balaam actually carried on a conversation with it. Because of this miracle, Balaam wasn't able to compromise with the enemy of God's people.

The prophet Elijah demonstrated the working of miracles. God raised a widow's son from the dead. First Kings 17:19–23 says,

> And he said unto her, Give me thy son. And he took him out of her bosom, and carried him up into a loft, where he abode, and laid him upon his own bed. And he cried unto the Lord, and said, O Lord my God, hast thou also brought evil upon the widow with whom I sojourn, by slaying her son? And he stretched himself upon the child three times, and cried unto the Lord, and said, O Lord my God, I pray thee, let this child's soul come into him again. And the Lord heard the voice of Elijah; and the soul of the child came into him again, and he revived. And Elijah took the child,

and brought him down out of the chamber into
the house, and delivered him unto his mother: and
Elijah said, See, thy son liveth.

This miracle done through Elijah would be classified as
working of miracles. Elijah participated in the process, and he
prayed to the Lord. As he prayed, he lay on the child three times.
The Lord heard his prayer, and life was restored to the little boy.

Our normal reasoning is that the boy is dead; we must bury
him. God's power through Elijah made an abnormal situation
normal again. God intervened on behalf of Elijah and the child.
The law of nature was changed.

In John 2:1–10, Jesus had creative powers. He and His disciples
were at a wedding feast, where the wedding couple ran out of wine.
Jesus told them to get six water pots and fill them with water. Upon
filling the water pots and the cups, the water turned into wine.

In John 6:1–12, Jesus fed a multitude of five thousand with
two fish and five loaves of bread. Not only did the five thousand
people eat until they were full, but twelve baskets of food were left
over for the disciples. Through the working of miracles, the law of
nature was affected.

The working of miracle isn't just in the realm of healing. God
can create a miracle in any aspects of our lives. We must believe
in miracles and that Jesus is a miracle worker.

A miracle is the power of God working through us for an
immediate cure. It will happen right now. God's miracle power can
cure an impossible situation. In the light of healing, a lot of people
pray for a healing, but they look for a miracle. Healings take place
over a process of time, whereas a miracle is immediate. God uses
the natural elements for His plan and purpose.

The gift of the working of miracles comprises the more
extraordinary and unusual kinds of miracles. In the working of
miracles, the laws of nature are altered or suspended. What is
abnormal to our natural reasoning is affected and made whole.

NOTES

CHAPTER 6
The Vocal Gifts

First Corinthians 12:10 says, "To another prophecy ... to another divers kinds of tongues; to another the interpretation of tongues." This group of gifts is called the gifts of inspiration. These gifts are designed so the church may grow in spiritual matters and be strong and powerful. They have a threefold mission: exhortation, edification, and comfort. The gift of prophecy is the greatest among these gifts (1 Cor. 11–14). We cannot operate in these gifts or any of the gifts of the Holy Spirit just because we want to. These gifts are given as the Holy Spirit wills. With the inspiration of the vocal gifts, we witness the power of words anointed by the Holy Spirit.

The Gift of Prophecy

The gift of prophecy produces a word spoken in the language where the recipient lives. It is a word from God given as the Holy Spirit wills. God, the Holy Spirit, will give a word to a believer to give to another, whether saved or not. A lot of people are prophesying to themselves. Some people have their own group of people they prophesy to. Not all words claimed to be prophecy are from God. Another, who is in the office of the prophet, should judge prophecy.

The purpose of the gift of prophecy is to edify, exhort, and comfort. First Corinthians 14:3 says, "But he that prophesieth speaketh unto men to edification, and exhortation, and comfort." The purpose isn't to condemn or judge. It is to build up the church and believers. We have a lot of parking lot prophecies. A parking lot prophecy is a person meeting a believer after worship and after the anointing has lifted and give a believer what they "feel" is a prophecy. This action can ultimately divide a church or put a believer's life in shambles. The gift of prophecy doesn't predict the future, but it should do one of these three purposes, if not all three.

When the Holy Spirit leads a believer to prophesy, this act doesn't make that person a prophet. A prophet is one of the ministry gifts given to the church. Ephesians 4:11 says, "And he gave some, apostles; and some, prophets; and some, evangelists; and some, pastors and teachers."

He is a person and not a vocal gift. In the book of Acts, Philip's daughters prophesied, but that doesn't mean they were prophets. Act 21:9 says, "And the same man had four daughters, virgins, which did prophesy."

They had the simple gift of prophecy, intended to edify, exhort, and comfort. A person called to the office of prophet has deeper spiritual insight and can foretell. The prophet in this office can tell more than what is on the surface.

Many have misused the gift of prophecy by giving guidance. The purpose of the gift of prophecy isn't guidance. It isn't preaching. Preaching is a divine declaration of the gospel of Jesus Christ. Preaching takes studying the word of God and the intellect. The gift of prophecy is an utterance in English that comes from one's most inner part, where God is speaking a right-now word. Someone must prepare to preach, whereas prophecy is unprepared. It is given through the unction of the Holy Spirit. First John 2:20 says, "But ye have an unction from the Holy One, and ye know all things."

The gift of prophecy is always encouraging and not rebuking. Some people are quick to rebuke a believer based on what they have heard and then want to say, "God has said" or "Thus saith the Lord." Criticizing another believer isn't a gift. The gift of prophecy can help a person out of depression, negligence, lukewarmness, and so forth and then bring him or her back in line with the Lord.

The purpose of the gift of prophecy is to edify (Greek, *oikodome*). The word *edify* means to build up, pointing to the act of building. Prophecy helps strengthen the weak. If someone has fear in his or her life, it will remove that fear. The way our world is today, people need this inspirational gift and encouragement. Many are depressed, dismayed, stressed, and suicidal. The Holy Spirit will send a supernatural utterance to break the yoke of bondage.

The purpose of the gift of prophecy is to exhort (Greek, *paraklesis*). The word *exhort* means to encourage. During the times when the devil discourages the church or an individual, the Lord sends a word of encouragement. The Holy Spirit will speak forcibly with encouragement. When a person or church doesn't feel it can't move forward, a prophecy will come: "Don't give up. Your breakthrough is knocking at the door."

The purpose of the gift of prophecy is to give comfort (Greek, *paramuthia*). It is intended for the purpose of persuading, calming, or consoling. Throughout the world today, we have hurting people. Some people are so dismayed that they don't know which way to turn. People come to church with their broken hearts. They need a word of comfort. Jesus said, "He will mend the brokenhearted" Lk. 4:18 Christians have broken dreams and broken homes, and their innermost beings are grieved. They need to be comforted and not judged.

You should always make sure your message of prophecy is of God. There are familiar spirits in operation that want to use you to prophesy. Familiar spirits will imitate prophecy. If it is a thought or something you have been thinking, don't say it. If it is a word that is deep down in your spirit, let it boil up and come out of you.

> There are, it may be, so many kinds of voices in the world, and none of them is without signification.
> (1 Cor. 14:10)

> Beloved, believe not every spirit, but try the spirits whether they are of God: because many false prophets are gone out into the world. (1 John 4:1)

Diverse Kinds of Tongues

This gift of the Holy Spirit is the most controversial one of our time. Many scholars have different views of this gift. Some scholars say it is an utterance of a *known language* given by the Holy Spirit. This is an unlearned language, but the believer is able to speak it. The other view is that the Holy Spirit gives an *unknown language*. The latter of the two views points toward our private devotion. My position on this gift is that it is a known language spoken and given by the Holy Spirit. This sign gift of diverse kinds of tongues is a supernatural utterance God gives through the Holy Spirit. This gift has nothing to do with people's intellect but comes through the spiritual part of people and manifests as a language.

The gift of diverse kinds of tongues is a public ministry, a sign gift for unbelievers. First Corinthians 14:22 says, "Wherefore tongues are for a sign, not to them that believe, but to them that believe not."

There may be an unsaved foreigner in the church. The Lord wants to save that individual, so He, the Holy Spirit, will cause a believer to utter words in the native language of the unbeliever. This was done on the day of Pentecost.

> And when the day of Pentecost was fully come, they were all with one accord in one place. And suddenly there came a sound from heaven as of a rushing mighty wind, and it filled all the house where they were sitting. And there appeared unto them cloven tongues like as of fire, and it sat upon each of them. And they were all filled with the Holy Ghost, and began to speak with other

> tongues, as the Spirit gave them utterance. And
> there were dwelling at Jerusalem Jews, devout men,
> out of every nation under heaven. Now when this
> was noised abroad, the multitude came together,
> and were confounded, because that every man
> heard them speak in his own language. (Acts
> 2:1–6)

The disciples were praying in one accord in the upper room. The Spirit of the Lord suddenly and unexpectedly came down like a rushing, mighty wind and descended on them like cloven fire. They were all filled with the Holy Ghost and began to speak with other tongues.

There were Jews from all over who came to Jerusalem for the Passover. When they heard the Galileans speak, they heard them speak in their native language. When the Holy Spirit anoints believers to speak, they have no idea what they're saying.

The infilling of the Holy Spirit brings this gift and all other gifts about. The infilling of the Spirit happens many times throughout the believer's life, whereas the baptism of the Holy Spirit is a one-time occurrence that happens at the moment of salvation.

The purpose of this gift is to edify, to build up, the church. The joy and excitement of the manifestation of the gift of tongues in an assembly confirm the word of God. They show the infilling of the Holy Spirit. Acts 10:45–47 says, "And they of the circumcision which believed were astonished, as many as came with Peter, because that on the Gentiles also was poured out the gift of the Holy Ghost. For they heard them speak with tongues, and magnify God. Then answered Peter, Can any man forbid water, that these should not be baptized, which have received the Holy Ghost as well as we?"

The apostle Peter went to Cornelius's house and began to proclaim the gospel of Jesus Christ: the death, burial, and resurrection. As Peter was preaching, the Holy Spirit came upon the Gentiles, and they began to speak with tongues and magnify God.

The Holy Spirit will raise the unknown tongue in us. This gift is for the believer's private life and devotion. When we speak in an unknown tongue, we speak out of our spirits to God. The Holy Spirit will bring the utterance out of our bellies. When our spirits are speaking, our minds are unfruitful in understanding. First Corinthians 14:14 says, "For if I pray in an unknown tongue, my spirit prayeth, but my understanding is unfruitful."

Deep down in our inner man comes the utterance. We can be in the midst of praying or glorying God, and our minds entertain the words "Thank You, Jesus," but when we open our mouths to say, "Thank You, Jesus," some syllables or an ecstatic utterance comes out. This unknown language or tongue takes time to learn and grow. This gift cannot be taught. We may grab the first few utterances, and the Spirit of the Lord gives us more. After a while, we learn to use them in our private lives.

Speaking in an unknown tongue builds or edifies the speaker. When we pray in the spirit, we pray to God and not to men. The apostle Paul often prayed in an unknown tongue. First Corinthians 14:18 says, "I thank my God, I speak with tongues more than ye all."

When we pray in our own prayer language, there is no need for anyone else. We speak to God no matter where we are. When we pray in tongues, we supernaturally pray out of our spirits. We can magnify God and sing songs and psalms to the Lord. Jude wrote to the church, "But ye, beloved, building up yourselves on your most holy faith, praying in the Holy Ghost" (Jude 1:20). Ephesians 5:18–19 says, "And be not drunk with wine, wherein is excess; but be filled with the Spirit; Speaking to yourselves in psalms and hymns and spiritual songs, singing and making melody in your heart to the Lord."

This is a form of worshiping God in spirit and in truth. Sometimes while praying in English, we tend to find other thoughts interjected in our minds. When praying in the Spirit with tongues, thoughts cannot come because our spirits pray and not our minds. Praying in English doesn't mean the Lord hasn't or won't hear our prayers. What it does mean is that our spirit prays. When our spirit prays, there are no interferences now or later.

Praying in an unknown tongue, we can intercede for others. A lot of time someone can be on our minds. We really don't know what to pray for. Praying in the spirit allows us to pray for that person. Romans 8:26 says, "Likewise the Spirit also helpeth our infirmities: for we know not what we should pray for as we ought: but the Spirit itself maketh intercession for us with groanings which cannot be uttered."

The Holy Spirit will guide and pray for us. He will help us in our infirmities. We can have tribulation on every hand, and we don't know how to pray as we ought. In the midst of praying, we praise God. The Holy Spirit knows the will of the Father and the heart of man. Through prayer in an unknown tongue, we achieve victories like never before.

There are many in the body of Christ who aren't sure about this gift. It takes boldness to operate in this gift. The question I propose to you is, what do you have to lose? We have everything to gain when we allow our spirit man or woman to pray.

The Interpretation of Tongues

The gift of the interpretation of tongues provides a supernatural presentation of a message in a known tongue for the message spoken in an unknown tongue. The interpreter doesn't know what was said. He or she just interprets what was said. When the Holy Spirit leads a person, he or she will give a message in the language of those present. When a message is given in an unknown tongue in a public form, one should be there to interpret it. The interpretation of tongues edifies the church. It is vital and necessity that, when a message is given in tongues, it is interpreted.

First Corinthians 14:13 says, "Wherefore let him that speaketh in an unknown tongue pray that he may interpret."

The interpretation of tongues isn't a translation of the message. The interpretation gives the meaning of the message. The message of the spoken tongue can be long, while the interpretation can be short. The interpretation can be long while the message spoken in an unknown tongue can be short. The interpretation comes by the Holy Spirit and not through the mind. There are some who have the gift of speaking in tongues or unknown tongue and also the gift of interpretation.

Most times the interpreter doesn't understand the language of the message. When someone gives the interpretation of the tongue, the Holy Spirit may give only one or two words at first. When the interpreter starts to interpret by faith, the Holy Spirit lets the rest of the message flow. The interpretation can come one of two ways: by words of inspiration or by the person seeing it develop in a vision. The gift of tongues, when spoken in a public form, should always have an interpreter. If an interpreter isn't there, the speaker of the language should hold his or her peace.

> I thank my God, I speak with tongues more than ye all: Yet in the church I had rather speak five words with my understanding, that by my voice I might teach others also, than ten thousand words in an unknown tongue. (1 Cor. 14:18–19)

> But if there be no interpreter, let him keep silence in the church; and let him speak to himself, and to God. (1 Cor. 14:28)

The church has no benefit if an unknown is uttered when there is no interpreter. God does things decently and in order. The Lord is about unity in the body of Christ, and He is no respecter of persons. The body of Christ isn't centered on one person on earth. The only person who is the center and head is Christ. First Corinthians 14:2 says, "For he that speaketh in an unknown tongue speaketh not unto men, but unto God: for no man understandeth him; howbeit in the spirit he speaketh mysteries."

The gift of tongues and the interpretation of tongues equal prophecy. We discussed earlier that prophecy edifies, exhorts, and comforts the body of Christ. So it is when these gifts are in operation that we have edification, exhortation, and comfort. These are two ways God has us doing the same thing. Prophecy speaks to the church, and a message in tongues speaks to the sinner. God uses these gifts to get a message out supernaturally by and through His Spirit.

All nine of these gifts of the Holy Spirit are given as He wills. We believers must have the faith that He will use us in this area of ministry. If you desire to have any of these gifts or all of them, read aloud, mediate on them, and ask the Holy Spirit to use you with His gifts. All the gifts of the Holy Spirit are yours for the asking. God is looking for willing vessels. He wants to use you, so you should make yourself available to Him.

NOTES

CHAPTER 7
Auxiliary Gifts

Auxiliary gifts are supporting gifts. Many of these gifts in many ways give support to those who have the ministry gifts or what some call the fivefold ministry. Some of the gifts are geared toward personal devotion and devotion to God, such as the gift of celibacy. Some gifts are for the edifying of the church. These gifts are just as important as any of the major gifts written herein or in the Holy Bible. Everyone will look at the person out front, but if things aren't running smoothly in the background, it will show out front. Although these are supporting gifts, they are all given so God will be glorified, the church will be edified, and the world will be evangelized.

Helps

The gift of helps can be twofold. The gift of helps and service are so closely related that we will look at both together. The gift of helps can be an administrative assistant, one who assists an individual or serves the church at large. The Greek word for "help" is *antilempseis*. It properly denotes aid, assistance, help; those who render aid, assistance, or help; helpers.

The gift of helps is a low-visible position but is just as important as any of the other gifts of the Holy Spirit. The gift of helps has a broad sense of ministry. It can cover in the narrow sense of being an administrative assistant to one serving the church or of serving the community as a whole.

Assistants to the leader would have the best interest of the leader and his vision. They are there to meet the needs of the leader. When the leader needs to meditate on his sermon, the helper will make sure he isn't disturbed. A pastor or speaker may need an errand run; the helper will see to getting it done. The assistant will learn everything about the leader and be his or her faithful protector.

Those leaders who mostly write books or newspaper articles have ghostwriters. A ghostwriter is the one who writes the details for the author or even writes the whole book based on the author's main ideal. Helpers can be of assistance in a lot of ways.

Moses had Aaron, and Elijah had Elisha.

> And Moses told Aaron all the words of the Lord who had sent him, and all the signs which he had commanded him. And Moses and Aaron went and gathered together all the elders of the children of Israel: And Aaron spake all the words which the Lord had spoken unto Moses, and did the signs in the sight of the people. (Ex. 4:28–30)

> So he departed thence, and found Elisha the son of Shaphat, who was plowing with twelve yoke of oxen before him, and he with the twelfth: and Elijah passed by him, and cast his mantle upon him. (1 Kings 19:19)

There are several occasions when the apostle Paul spoke of his helpers in the ministry. He traveled throughout Asia and Jerusalem, and he planted many churches by spreading the gospel of Jesus Christ. The apostle Paul had Barnabas to accompany him while on his mission journey. Every leader in the church needs a helper. No leader can do everything alone. The work of the ministry is too big and complicated for one person to do it all. Often the church suffers because of the lack of help in the church. Many members are neglected because of the solo act. Many pastors and leaders in the church are stressed out and stretched out because they feel or want to do everything themselves. Contrary to popular belief, pastors or leaders of a church, ministry, or auxiliary can get more done if they use the proper helper or helpers in the church or ministry.

> I commend unto you Phebe our sister, which is a servant of the church which is at Cenchrea: That ye receive her in the Lord, as becometh saints, and that ye assist her in whatsoever business she hath need of you: for she hath been a succourer of many, and of myself also. (Rom. 16:1–2)

> Greet Priscilla and Aquila my helpers in Christ Jesus. (Rom. 16:3)

> Salute Urbane, our helper in Christ, and Stachys my beloved. (Rom. 16:9)

Those who have the gift of helps in a broader sense serve the church at large. They aid in the temporal affairs of the church, caring for the poor or the distribution of charity, whether it is monetary, a food pantry, and so forth. These believers are those who are profitable and useful in various ways to take care of the spiritual welfare of the church. Usually those with the gift of helps to oversee spiritual welfare are the elders, deacons, or deaconesses of the church or those who have compassion for God's people and passion for kingdom building.

Believers who have the gift of helps will volunteer to visit those in prisons and hospitals, help the homeless, and meet the needs of the seniors, widows, and children throughout the congregation and community. It is the Christian's duty and ministry to visit those less fortunate than we are, whom God has blessed. Jesus has called all believers to do the work of the ministry.

Matthew 25:34–36 says, "Then shall the King say unto them on his right hand, Come, ye blessed of my Father, inherit the kingdom prepared for you from the foundation of the world: For I was an hungred, and ye gave me meat: I was thirsty, and ye gave me drink: I was a stranger, and ye took me in: Naked, and ye clothed me: I was sick, and ye visited me: I was in prison, and ye came unto me."

In Exodus 18:13–27, we read that Moses counseled the children of Israel from sunup to sundown. The people lined up with their problems, and Moses told them what the commandments of God would say and judge the matters. Moses's father-in-law, Jethro, saw what Moses was doing and how it would be devastating to him and God's chosen ones. Jethro suggested that Moses get "able men, such as fear God, men of truth, hating covetousness; and place such over them, to be rulers of thousands, and rulers of hundreds, rulers of fifties, and rulers of tens" (Ex. 18:21). Moses adhered to the voice of his father-in-law and picked men from each tribe to represent him. They handled the small matters of the people and brought the major matters to Moses to judge. In doing so, there was peace among the people as well as Moses.

> If thou shalt do this thing, and God command thee so, then thou shalt be able to endure, and all this people shall also go to their place in peace. (Ex. 18:23)

> And they judged the people at all seasons: the hard causes they brought unto Moses, but every small matter they judged themselves. (Ex 18:26)

> And the Lord said unto Moses, Gather unto me seventy men of the elders of Israel, whom thou knowest to be the elders of the people, and officers over them; and bring them unto the tabernacle of the congregation, that they may stand there with thee. And I will come down and talk with thee there: and I will take of the spirit which is upon thee, and will put it upon them; and they shall bear the burden of the people with thee, that thou bear it not thyself alone. (Num. 11:16–17)

Here Moses led almost three million to the Promised Land. Moses had to see to the care and problems of the children of Israel, but since he was the sole leader, the task had become too much for him to bear. He prayed and pleaded with the Lord, even to the extent that he asked the Lord to take his life. So the Lord had Moses gather seventy elders of Israel to help him. When the Lord communed with Moses, He took the spirit that had been on Moses and put it on the seventy elders.

Moses appointed the elders and gave them instructions for what their tasks would be, but it was the Lord who equipped the elders for service. In light of the aforementioned passage, there are some in the church who are already serving the people, but they can also be given a greater task. As the task is given, the Lord will equip them with His Spirit. Acts 6:3–6 says, "Wherefore, brethren, look ye out among you seven men of honest report, full of the Holy Ghost and wisdom, whom we may appoint over this business. But we will give ourselves continually to prayer, and to the ministry of the word. And the saying pleased the whole multitude: and they chose Stephen, a man full of faith and of the Holy Ghost, and Philip, and Prochorus, and Nicanor, and Timon, and Parmenas, and Nicolas a proselyte of Antioch: Whom they set before the apostles: and when they had prayed, they laid their hands on them."

The twelve apostles were going about and preaching the word of God as Jesus Christ had commanded them to do. In the meantime, there developed murmurings among the Greeks, who complained against the Jews. The complaint was that the Jews were neglecting the Greek widows in the daily ministration of the church.

Since the apostle couldn't be there full-time, they asked the disciples of the church to appoint seven men, full of the Holy Spirit and wisdom, to take care of the church's welfare. The church picked out the seven men, and the apostles laid hands on them to carry out the task before them.

Governments

The word *government* comes from the word *kuberiao*. *Kuberiao* means "to govern or steer a ship." This gift regards those who have skills and talents for doing business. They are those who can thoughtfully direct the affairs of the church. They handle the business of the church in accordance with the pastor's vision. Most of these people are those some call trustees, stewards, deacon, elders, advisers, or the like. One doesn't have to be on a delegated council to be part of the building of the kingdom of God as such, but it would be suitable to be so.

This position in the church or ministry isn't a permanent office. The most important attribute is being able to pull together the plan for the ministry or church. People may come and go, but the work business continues. There is a need for many to serve in this capacity for the advancement of the body of Christ. This area of ministry or church work causes one to have a deep and comprehensive mind, one who is wise and prudent in the care of the church's welfare. The ones gifted with governing aren't called to this position, but God set them in the church, and the pastor appoints them.

Luke 14:28–30 says, "For which of you, intending to build

a tower, sitteth not down first, and counteth the cost, whether he have sufficient to finish it? Lest haply, after he hath laid the foundation, and is not able to finish it, all that behold it begin to mock him, Saying, This man began to build, and was not able to finish." Here Christ the Lord was conversing with His disciples to render to them the cost of discipleship and kingdom building. A good steward or one in the position of governing the business of the church or ministry will explore every avenue for the vision. Those in this position will weigh the cost, time, and plan to complete the immediate and long-term projects. The caution rendered to those who have this gift is not to rely solely on their gifts, talents, or skills; instead, they should yield to the Holy Spirit's guidance. Not everyone can be put in these positions, even if he or she does have what it takes. He or she must have certain characteristics.

The trustees or stewards who handle church business must be of an honest report, full of the Holy Ghost and wisdom, not given to filthy lucre, slow to anger, and holding to the faith. When we have men and women of the faith handling church business, there is a better chance that it will be done with honesty and integrity. Therefore, when those of good report handle the affairs, they will leave the pastor to meditate on the word of God and minister to the people of God.

The Lord will give the vision to the pastor, but He will also put people in the local church to fulfill the vision or mission. Those whom the Lord sets in the church and the pastor appoints should have team-building skills. They should understand the pastor's vision and develop a plan to set it in motion. The pastor will give the ultimate goal, and the one in charge of the plan will get the church there. The person as such should develop a team to pursue the goal the pastor sets for the church. The chief administrator pays attention to details. The team of administrators will carry out the plan and be successful at it.

Titus 1:5 says, "For this cause left I thee in Crete, that thou shouldest set in order the things that are wanting, and ordain elders in every city, as I had appointed thee." Here the apostle Paul left Titus in Crete to finish the work he had started. Titus had been with the apostle for quite some time. They worked together to establish churches in Greece. The apostle Paul trained Titus, the minister, until they had the same mind and goal. Titus didn't deviate from the vision of the apostle Paul. Titus was left to do several tasks for Paul. He took care or ministered in the churches in Corinth.

Second Corinthians 8:23 says, "Whether any do enquire of Titus, he is my partner and fellowhelper concerning you: or our brethren be enquired of, they are the messengers of the churches, and the glory of Christ." Since Titus traveled with Paul and Paul knew what kind of person and minister he was, he trusted Titus with an awesome responsibility to complete. The apostle Paul left Titus in Crete to finish the work that had been started. The apostle didn't just leave him there, but he gave him instructions on the work and what to do. Chapters 2–3 present the instructions given to Titus for the advancement of the church and the kingdom of God.

Anyone given a task for the church, ministry, or organization should do so as if the leader were doing it. The person in government should make sure the vision of the leader is completed to the best of his or her ability.

Leadership
Romans 12:8

What is leadership? A leader is one who is set over others and presides with diligence and care for something. Leadership can cover various headships from the head of a family, organizations, auxiliaries, churches, ministries, and so forth. There is a difference between "driver ship" and leadership. When one is a leader of any sort, driving people with an iron fist or dictatorship is demeaning and far less effective than leadership.

Driver ship causes one to be manipulative and mandate certain results. Often you may get a result but not the results you need. They will bring about discontented lay leaders, administrators, and so forth. Driver ship causes fear rather than love and happiness. Would you rather someone do a task out of love or fear? Even more so, would you rather someone respect you out of love or fear? Driver ship doesn't take in consideration the views of other people. The views of the leader who drives the people are the only ones that matters. They are very selfish and opinionated. Some dictators don't care how they get respect as long as they get it. To get respect in a negative manner reflects on the character and history of the person in charge. Leadership, on the other hand, is the total opposite.

The person in leadership is one who leads by example. Leadership methods are tactful and meek. The meek leader's actions speak louder than his or her words. A good person may be meek, but that doesn't mean he or she is weak. A lot of people mistake meekness for weakness. A person in leadership knows when to be tender as a lamb and when to roar like a lion. Matthew 11:29 says, "Take my yoke upon you, and learn of me; for I am meek and lowly in heart: and ye shall find rest unto your souls."

One of the characteristics of Christ was meekness. To be meek is to be gentle, hospitable toward others, but firm when the occasion calls for it. A leader of such service tends to get more accomplished, and the people will be glad to do it. How leaders talk to people can make a difference in how others respond to them. Jesus Christ was gentle with His disciples, but when the situations called for Him to be firm with them, He did just that. A person leading by example will stand for what is right and not just go with the flow. Matthew 21:12–13 says, "And Jesus went into the temple of God, and cast out all them that sold and bought in the temple, and overthrew the tables of the moneychangers, and the seats of them that sold doves, And said unto them, It is written, My house shall be called the house of prayer; but ye have made it a den of thieves."

A person in leadership should have the charisma to pull people together to accomplish a goal. He or she values the opinion of others. The leader doesn't always have the best ideas. Some people whom God has gifted can have a better way of getting their goals accomplished.

Let's look at the leadership of the church or ministry. First and foremost, Jesus Christ Himself has appointed the head of the church. Ephesians 4:11 says, "And he gave some, apostles; and some, prophets; and some, evangelists; and some, *pastors* and teachers" (emphasis added). It is He, Jesus Christ.

The pastor should be Holy Spirit led for the vision of the church. Likewise, the trustees, deacons, stewards, and so forth, whom the pastor has appointed, would help fulfill the vision Christ gave to the pastor. The teamwork concept is a good way to get various ideas and opinions to accomplish the vision of the church. Jesus had a ministry team carry on the work of the ministry or church.

Every church needs people with the gift of helps in this area of ministry. The pastor should be free to meditate and minister the word of God freely without any undue stress. The people appointed must be honest and led by the Holy Spirit. If the Holy Spirit and wisdom lead those who are appointed, one can rest assured that the congregation will be taken care of and no one will be neglected. Acts 6:3–4 says, "Wherefore, brethren, look ye out among you seven men of honest report, full of the Holy Ghost and wisdom, whom we may appoint over this business. But we will give ourselves continually to prayer, and to the ministry of the word."

There was a problem in the Jerusalem church. The apostles couldn't be there on a continual bases. Therefore, they needed help to meet the needs of the church. They put out a request that the people of the church should pick seven men of good report to minister to the congregation. They would carry on the work and care of the people while the apostles would give themselves to prayer and the word of God.

No leader can do all the planning and executing. There have

been a lot of churches, ministry, auxiliaries, committees, and so forth that have suffered or become stagnant because the leader tried to do it all. Any organization of the church or ministry will prosper when there is teamwork and everyone is doing his or her part cheerfully.

> For this cause left I thee in Crete, that thou shouldest set in order the things that are wanting, and ordain elders in every city, as I had appointed thee. (Titus 1:5)

> As I besought thee to abide still at Ephesus, when I went into Macedonia, that thou mightest charge some that they teach no other doctrine, Neither give heed to fables and endless genealogies, which minister questions, rather than godly edifying which is in faith. (1 Tim. 1:3–4; compare to 1 Tim. 15:17; Heb. 13:17).

Earlier, we looked at this scripture from Titus's standpoint. Now let's look at it from the apostle Paul's view. Paul could leave Titus in Crete, because Titus had a proved ministry and leadership qualities. The apostle had trained Titus to be of the same mind and mission. As one is in a leadership position, we must learn to steer others toward the fulfillment of the overall vision of the church, ministry, or organization. Paul couldn't be everywhere at the same time or meet the need of the different churches he established. Therefore, he set others in place to fulfill the mission Christ had set in order in Matthew 28:19–20 and Mark 16:15–18.

Mercy

What is mercy? Mercy is defined as the ability to have not only empathy or sympathy but also compassion for someone, whether by word or deed. When an individual needs something, it isn't enough to just pray for him or her. The Lord has blessed us so we can be a blessing to other; He blesses others through us. The demonstration of compassion isn't just toward believers but also for unbelievers. It is universal and for all mankind. Compassion or mercy is extended for those not only with physical needs but also with mental and emotional needs.

Mercy is the ability to bring hope and turn sorrow into joy through the love of Christ. Jesus spoke to His disciples about compassion on earth and accountability before His throne (Matt. 25:34–40). The ministry and area of compassion given in Matthew 25 are for believers and unbelievers. Paul expressed the desire to go to Jerusalem to help the poor saints there. He petitioned the believers at Macedonia and Achaia for contributions for those who were less fortunate and stood in need of help. As children of God, we help others not only in spiritual matters but also in carnal ones. Romans 15:25–27 says, "But now I go unto Jerusalem to minister unto the saints. For it hath pleased them of Macedonia and Achaia to make a certain contribution for the poor saints which are at Jerusalem. It hath pleased them verily; and their debtors they are. For if the Gentiles have been made partakers of their spiritual things, their duty is also to minister unto them in carnal things."

In the parable of the Good Samaritan, Jesus spoke to the lawyer concerning who our neighbor is. Thieves had ambushed a man and left him for dead. On two different occasions, a priest and Levite saw this man lying on the side of the rode, but they walked on the other side of the street. A stranger, who wasn't a religious figure, came and dressed the man's wounds, led him to a place of safety, paid for his stay at a hotel, and promised to return and pay for any other expenses. Any person in spiritual or physical need is our neighbor (Luke 10:33–37).

The act of mercy has a two-edge sword. We must give mercy to obtain mercy. There may be a time or times when we would want someone to extend mercy or compassion in our lives. We show mercy toward others as an act of love from God. Christ shows mercy to us as we show mercy to others. It's truly a blessing when we bless or help others physically, mentally or emotionally. Matthew 5:7 says, "Blessed are the merciful: for they shall obtain mercy."

Exhortation

Roman 12:8 says, "Or he that exhorteth, on exhortation: he that giveth, let him do it with simplicity; he that ruleth, with diligence; he that sheweth mercy, with cheerfulness."

The person gifted with exhortation gives comfort, encouragement, and consolation. The results are that when one gives wisdom to others, the recipient will feel helped, healed, and set at liberty. A person would be able to recognize those who are distraught. Life can throw curve balls into our lives that can be stressful, burdensome, and overwhelming. God put people in our lives with this gift to help us through these tough times. Sometimes just a hug of comfort does a lot for an individual. The unspoken words are just as helpful as ten thousand spoken words. There are many who want to give up and throw in the towel, but when we exhort one another, we will encourage and strengthen someone to keep going. Acts 14:22 says, "Confirming the souls of the disciples, and exhorting them to continue in the faith, and that we must through much tribulation enter into the kingdom of God."

I recall a situation I encountered when I had to exhort a believer. There was a young lady at a church I once attended who always had a smile on her face. She seemed to be so happy all the time. On one particular Sunday, we were at church. She, my sister, and a couple of other people were standing in the vestibule. She was smiling and talking like she was glad to be at church. As I was observed her, I had unction in my spirit that something was going on with her.

I asked the young lady, "How are you doing?"

She replied, "I am blessed and highly favored!"

"But now how do you really feel?"

She looked at me and started crying. I pulled her aside and asked my sister to give her a hug. Behind her lovely smile was a hurting heart.

Exhortation isn't of our own strength or about us at all. It doesn't require or induce others to rely on their own strength, but it directs them to the love and healing power of Jesus Christ. Often a person feels alone, like nobody cares. The storms of life and attacks of the enemy can cause others to waver. Not only is the person with the gift of exhortation able to discern someone who has an issue of the heart, but there are some who are also professional counselors. They have the secular and educational knowledge as well as biblical knowledge and spiritual truths. They can help those who have problems to acknowledge those in the natural realm so they may also be healed in the spirit realm.

In Matthew 9:2–6, Jesus healed a paralyzed man but recognized he needed to be healed from the inside out. Therefore, he told the man his sins were forgiven and to take up his bed and walk. Thus, as Jesus did with this man, so can one who has the gift of exhortation do as a professional counselor. Therefore, as those with the gift of exhortation remind others of God and His love, they are never alone.

> For God hath not given us the spirit of fear; but of power, and of love, and of a sound mind. (2 Tim. 1:7)

> Or he that exhorteth, on exhortation: he that giveth, let him do it with simplicity; he that ruleth, with diligence; he that sheweth mercy, with cheerfulness. (Rom. 12:8)

> Confirming the souls of the disciples, and
> exhorting them to continue in the faith, and that
> we must through much tribulation enter into the
> kingdom of God. (Acts 14:22)

Exhortation is given not only to individuals but also corporately to a congregation. Churches within the body of Christ suffer many things. There are tactics of Satan against a church, tactics such as division, strife, envy, animosity, and the like. Pastors and their congregations become discouraged and need to be encouraged. Thus, God will send someone their way to impart encouragement to them, whether through the preached word, songs of praise and worship, or inspired words of reassurance. Hebrews 10:25 says, "Not forsaking the assembling of ourselves together, as the manner of some is; but exhorting one another: and so much the more, as ye see the day approaching."

There are times when a church collectively believes God for certain projects to come to pass, but it just seems like they aren't coming together or not happening, including the roadblocks put in the way or the many obstacles lying in the path. When a church's faith is tested, some members need exhortation. In modern times, the body of Christ needs exhortation, edification, and comfort now more than ever. Christendom is under attack with mockery and subtle persecution. As reflecting in the days of Herod Agrippa, who vexed or persecuted certain of the church, we are quickly returning to those days, and it is closer to us than you may think. We who are of the body of Christ have a hold on our profession of faith regardless of the circumstances. The Lord reigns and is in control of all things. We must continue to spread the gospel of Jesus Christ to the world.

> And many other things in his exhortation
> preached he (Jesus) unto the people. (Luke 3:18)

> And after the reading of the law and the prophets the rulers of the synagogue sent unto them, saying, Ye men and brethren, if ye have any word of exhortation for the people, say on. (Acts 13:15)

> But he that prophesieth speaketh unto men to edification, and exhortation, and comfort. He that speaketh in an unknown tongue edifieth himself; but he that prophesieth edifieth the church. (1 Cor. 14:3–4)

Giving

Romans 12:8 says, "Or he that exhorteth, on exhortation: he that giveth, let him do it with simplicity; he that ruleth, with diligence; he that sheweth mercy, with cheerfulness." It is every believer's responsibility or stewardship to give to his or her local church. God has given us a systematic way to give, and the beginning of it is tithes and offerings. Ten percent of our gross earnings go toward the business aspect of the church. Whether a believer is rich or poor, he or she should give tithes and offerings to the church. Believers of the church are skeptical about giving their tithes to the church, but if you trust God with your tithes and offerings, He will bless you as He promised in the book of Malachi. The tithes and offerings are for the advancement of the kingdom of God.

> Bring ye all the tithes into the storehouse, that there may be meat in mine house, and prove me now herewith, saith the Lord of hosts, if I will not open you the windows of heaven, and pour you out a blessing, that there shall not be room enough to receive it. (Mal. 3:10)

And Jesus sat over against the treasury, and beheld
how the people cast money into the treasury: and
many that were rich cast in much. And there
came a certain poor widow, and she threw in two
mites, which make a farthing. And he called unto
him his disciples, and saith unto them, Verily I say
unto you, That this poor widow hath cast more in,
than all they which have cast into the treasury:
For all they did cast in of their abundance; but she
of her want did cast in all that she had, even all
her living. (Mark 12:41–44)

Those who have the gift of giving are those God gifted to give
of their resources cheerfully and freely. These are those who give of
their financial resources for the work of the church. They usually
give above and beyond their tithes and offerings. Because of their
willingness and cheerfulness, God blesses them even more. It is
through material blessings that one is able to give of his or her
material assets. Those with the gift of giving are unselfish. They
give first and foremost so God would be glorified and the church
would be edified. They don't give to receive prestige or recognition;
they want to see the church succeed.

The apostle Paul requested that the churches in Macedonia give
beyond their average giving, whether they were rich or poor. This
was for the sake of those in need at Jerusalem. In his letter to the
church in Corinth, he encouraged them to give as those who were
in Macedonia. He expressed that God loves a cheerful giver. Those
who have the gift of giving do so cheerfully and not grudgingly.
When God gives a person the gift of giving, it starts in the heart.
The apostle Paul gave a principle of sowing financial seed; "He which
soweth sparingly shall reap also sparingly; and he which soweth
bountifully shall reap also bountifully" (2 Cor. 9:6). As a person gives,
so will God restore and give an increase in his or her life.

Hospitality

Hospitality is an act or practice of receiving and entertaining strangers or guests without reward or with kind and generous liberality. Throughout the Bible, it speaks of believers being hospitable or kind toward one and another. In the Old Testament, the Lord gave laws as they related to how to treat strangers well as how to have compassion for the poor. In the book of Leviticus, the Lord reminded Israel that they were strangers in the land of Egypt. If a stranger were to come upon their land, the Hebrews weren't to trouble them but to treat and love them as family. Hospitality is a Jewish tradition. When someone, a visitor, would come into their home, they would wash the dust off their feet. Leviticus 19:33–34 says, "And if a stranger sojourn with thee in your land, ye shall not vex him. But the stranger that dwelleth with you shall be unto you as one born among you, and thou shalt love him as thyself; for ye were strangers in the land of Egypt: I am the Lord your God."

The land that God gave to Israelites had a great harvest. God commanded them that they weren't to forget the poor. They weren't to harden their hearts, but they were to give to the poor. Thus, the Lord gave them the land, and Israel couldn't afford to be selfish and should give to the poor sufficiently when they stood in need. This is the basic character and commandment the Lord bestowed on Israel. And so is it with the body of Christ; we must remember that all we have comes from the Lord. The Lord has the same mandate on us, the body of Christ, who have sufficient material possession to give to the poor. Deuteronomy 15:7 says, "If there be among you a poor man of one of thy brethren within any of thy gates in thy land which the Lord thy God giveth thee, thou shalt not harden thine heart, nor shut thine hand from thy poor brother."

We have the same mandate recorded in the New Testament. We should have compassion or hospitality toward others. The apostles wanted the churches to follow hospitality. The apostle

Peter encouraged the church to be kind toward one another without a grudge.

It is imperative that church greeters show hospitality to the guests who visit our churches. The greeters are the first ones with whom the guests come into contact. The impression greeters have on guests, from the parking lot to the church door, will have an impact on whether they will stay.

First Peter 4:9–10 says, "Use hospitality one to another without grudging. As every man hath received the gift, even so minister the same one to another, as good stewards of the manifold grace of God." God has given a person with the gift of hospitality the special ability to make others feel warm, welcome, and like family. Those who have the gift of hospitality are happy and feel fulfilled when exercising this gift. Those with this gift manifest it not only to people they know but more so to strangers. They show forth the glory and love of God toward others. They have the supernatural ability to make one feel welcome in his or her home or in the church. Most people don't have or acknowledge this gift in them, because most people don't want others in their home.

I have a friend who has the gift of hospitality. He loves to have others over for dinner or just for a good time. He really knows how to make his guests feel welcome and at home. He will cook, bake, barbecue, or do whatever it takes to make sure those who come have something they like to eat. He opens his doors to whosoever will come. As we enter the house, he or his wife greets us with the biggest smile and salutation.

Hospitality is very important and useful when it comes to church growth. It is important for fellowship, social events, and especially worship services. In our modern times, people want to feel warm and like family on these occasions. This experience gives believers and unbeliever alike a sense of belonging. People who have the gift of hospitality have a really nice and motivated personality. They would make sure the needs of the guests are met. The ones with the gift of hospitality will gladly make sure all guests who come to church receive information about the church and contact information. Church guests should walk away with confidence and a sense of experiencing God's love.

Missionary

Who are missionaries, and what are their mission? Missionaries are those who have the God-given responsibility to go to other countries or cultures and evangelize others with the gospel of Jesus Christ. There are very few within the body of Christ to whom the Lord has given this gift. Some haven't recognized that they have it. The gift requires a sacrifice on the part of the recipient. Compared to those who live in the United States or any other well-developed country, to go into a third-world or less-developed country and live there for an extended amount of time would require one to live with considerably less. We can borrow the words of the apostle Paul although he wasn't a stationary missionary that is to say to stay in one place, but an apostle on the move.

Philippians 4:11–12 says, "Not that I speak in respect of want: for I have learned, in whatsoever state I am, therewith to be content. I know both how to be abased, and I know how to abound: every where and in all things I am instructed both to be full and to be hungry, both to abound and to suffer need."

Those who have the gift of being a missionary enjoy not only spreading the gospel in other countries but also learning other cultures. They will go through the process of learning the culture of the country in which they will live for a long period. The enthusiasm of those with the gift drives them to learn the language and slang of the culture in which they are involved, to adapt to the environment, and to be accepted by the inhabitants. God has gifted them to truly adapt to different cultures.

I have a young friend, Terrence Cole, whom I believe has the gift of being a missionary. He loves to go to other countries and learn their cultures and languages. He spent some years in

Korea, New Zealand, and other countries. He loves to travel to other countries and stay awhile. He learned their languages rather quickly and speaks them fluently. He can speak and read Spanish and French, and he can speak Korean. He spent six months in Spain, one month in Mexico, three years in Korea, and six months in New Zealand. He visited Portugal, France, Thailand, and Japan. He spent time with other missionaries in Korea and New Zealand. He taught English to the Korean and Thai students of their local churches. He could be a gifted missionary, but he hasn't recognized this.

For three years in a row, I went to General Santos, Philippines, for two weeks in September. It is two hours south of Manila. We went there to do miracle crusades and church planting. I also taught the senior pastors there in leadership seminars. I didn't learn their language, so I had to get an interpreter. So does that say I have the gift of being a missionary? Not so much. I am more so an apostle.

The apostle Paul had the gifts of being both an apostle and a missionary. As an apostle, he operated in that office, and his missionary journey took him to different places. In some places he stayed for a couple of years, and in some places he stayed long enough to plant churches. Paul was called and then sent of God. He traveled all over the known regions of that time. He was a servant to all and became or identified with the culture he was trying to reach with the gospel. He became identifiable so he could gain or win them over for Christ. The example Paul set was the example and priority of the one gifted with being a missionary. The person must be touchable by the other cultures to touch them with the gospel of Jesus Christ.

> Now there were in the church that was at Antioch
> certain prophets and teachers; as Barnabas, and
> Simeon that was called Niger, and Lucius of
> Cyrene, and Manaen, which had been brought

up with Herod the tetrarch, and Saul. As they ministered to the Lord, and fasted, the Holy Ghost said, Separate me Barnabas and Saul for the work whereunto I have called them. And when they had fasted and prayed, and laid their hands on them, they sent them away. (Acts 13:1–3)

For though I be free from all men, yet have I made myself servant unto all, that I might gain the more. And unto the Jews I became as a Jew, that I might gain the Jews; to them that are under the law, as under the law, that I might gain them that are under the law; To them that are without law, as without law, (being not without law to God, but under the law to Christ,) that I might gain them that are without law. To the weak became I as weak, that I might gain the weak: I am made all things to all men, that I might by all means save some. And this I do for the gospel's sake, that I might be partaker thereof with you. (1 Cor. 9:19–23)

Worship Leader

A worship leader is more than a good singer or musician who leads the congregation in praise and worship. I have been to many churches that have praise teams, and the worship leader and musician missed the move of the Holy Spirit. The Holy Spirit created an atmosphere of worship, but the worship leader or musician started to sing or play praise music. The Holy Spirit will direct the worship service differently on any given occasion. Those who have the gift of leading worship should lead the worship service as the Holy Spirit leads. They have the God-given ability to draw others into experiencing God during the worship service.

They are sensitive to the directions and emphases of the Holy Spirit.

The Lord wants the worship leader to create an atmosphere in which the congregation will express their hearts to the Lord. Worship should be about more than people coming together; it should be about having an experience with God. Music is important to the worship experience. Through song, worship leaders can lead people to release themselves into adoration to the Lord. Just as any minister shouldn't preach without praying, the minister of music or worship leader, who sings or plays, shouldn't lead without prayer.

We must have the appropriate musical place for the ministry gifts to operate effectively (for example, prophesying, deliverance, spiritual warfare, and healings). When the worship leader and team are of one accord with the Holy Spirit and induce congregants to give of themselves in worship, they enhance the preaching of the gospel. First Samuel 10:5 says, "After that thou shalt come to the hill of God, where is the garrison of the Philistines: and it shall come to pass, when thou art come thither to the city, that thou shalt meet a company of prophets coming down from the high place with a psaltery, and a tabret, and a pipe, and a harp, before them; and they shall prophesy."

When the worship leader and his or her team are of one accord with the Holy Spirit, corporate praise and worship is enhanced, and the glory of the Lord will fill the place of worship. The historical books of the Old Testament speak primarily of the Levites and other singers who ushered in the presence of the Lord. The book of Psalms is a book of songs and prayers expressed toward God.

> Also the Levites which were the singers, all of them of Asaph, of Heman, of Jeduthun, with their sons and their brethren, being arrayed in white linen, having cymbals and psalteries and harps, stood at the east end of the altar, and with them

an hundred and twenty priests sounding with
trumpets: It came even to pass, as the trumpeters
and singers were as one, to make one sound to
be heard in praising and thanking the Lord; and
when they lifted up their voice with the trumpets
and cymbals and instruments of musick, and
praised the Lord, saying, For he is good; for his
mercy endureth for ever: that then the house was
filled with a cloud, even the house of the Lord;
So that the priests could not stand to minister by
reason of the cloud: for the glory of the Lord had
filled the house of God. (2 Chron. 5:12–14)

Intercession

Intercession or interceding is when individuals pray for someone,
an event, or an organization until they get results. In general,
every believer should pray and intercede for one another and for
the world. But when people have the gift of intercession, they are
specific in their prayers. They will labor in prayer for an hour or
hours for a specific thing or person. They are the ones who usually
get answers from their prayers more so than average believers. The
one who has the gift of intercession has a dual gift with the gift
of faith.

First Timothy 2:1–2 says, "I exhort therefore, that, first of all,
supplications, prayers, intercessions, and giving of thanks, be made
for all men; For kings, and for all that are in authority; that we may
lead a quiet and peaceable life in all godliness and honesty." The
apostle Paul exhorted apostle Timothy to pray for all and for his
ministry to spread the gospel peacefully throughout the region. It
is noteworthy that all churches or ministries would seek out those
who have the gift of intercession and form an intercessory team;
these people labor in prayer for the sake of the ministry and the
ongoing work of the church. Intercessors pray that the knowledge

of the Lord's will, wisdom, and spiritual growth would be upon the church.

Colossians 4:12 says, "Epaphras, who is one of you, a servant of Christ, saluteth you, always labouring fervently for you in prayers, that ye may stand perfect and complete in all the will of God." People who pray with such intensity and earnestly hear the voice of God more often and more regularly than the average Christian, who prays unselfishly. They have a humble and mature disposition in spirit and spiritual things. They gain a sense of satisfaction and joy to toil for the church and others. They toil with believing God will answer their prayers, and He does so in dramatic fashion.

James 5:14–16 says, "Is any sick among you? let him call for the elders of the church; and let them pray over him, anointing him with oil in the name of the Lord: And the prayer of faith shall save the sick, and the Lord shall raise him up; and if he have committed sins, they shall be forgiven him. Confess your faults one to another, and pray one for another, that ye may be healed. The effectual fervent prayer of a righteous man availeth much."

Celibacy

Celibacy is defined as a state of supreme sacrifice. God has gifted some to promise to themselves and the body of Christ that they will never indulge in any sexual activity. Those who practice abstinence for the Lord won't have their attention divided. A married person must balance time between family and ministry work. He or she has to plan family time and find time to take vacations, date nights or what is pleasing for your family. Most people desire to wed someday. After all, God constituted marriage at the beginning in the Garden of Eden.

Believers who have the gift of celibacy aren't singled out just to be single. They delight in being single and committed to the Lord. They are single for a purpose, and that purpose is for the Lord. Their sole purpose is to serve the Lord.

They have an advantage over most Christian. They are devoted to the Lord, and they don't have to allocate time to a spouse or immediate family. The apostle Paul spoke of this fact in 1 Corinthians 7. Theologians conclude that Paul was a widower. First Corinthians 7:7–8 says, "For I would that all men were even as I myself. But every man hath his proper gift of God, one after this manner, and another after that. I say therefore to the unmarried and widows, It is good for them if they abide even as I."

The apostle Paul was fully dedicated to spreading the gospel of Jesus Christ. The minds of believers who have the gift of celibacy are free of any unwanted desires and feelings. God will give them a pure state of mind. This gift is given only to a few people. Therefore, celibate believers can meditate, worship in their private devotion, and do the work of missionaries. Jesus addressed the devotion of singles by way of talking about eunuchs in the context of marriage. He gave examples of men born as eunuch, man-made eunuchs, and eunuchs who made themselves eunuchs for the sake of the kingdom. The third example, volunteer eunuchs, is used here for the gift of celibacy. Voluntary eunuchs are those who, to better serve the Lord in some capacity, choose to forego marriage and fully devote themselves to the Lord.

Matthew 19:11–12 says, "But he said unto them, All men cannot receive this saying, save they to whom it is given. For there are some eunuchs, which were so born from their mother's womb: and there are some eunuchs, which were made eunuchs of men: and there be eunuchs, which have made themselves eunuchs for the kingdom of heaven's sake. He that is able to receive it, let him receive it."

Voluntary Poverty

The gift of voluntary poverty is given to some believers in the body of Christ who voluntarily give up their possessions and adopt a lifestyle level of social poverty to do a service for the Lord.

In contrast, there is a difference between those who volunteer poverty and those who are living in poverty dictated by societal circumstances. Those who have the gift of volunteer poverty become identifiable or touchable to those who don't have much at all. They will live among them and reach out to them with the love of Christ. I so often see believers within the body of Christ fully dressed in suits and ties, dresses, the normal church attire evangelizing those who doesn't have much and living in poverty. Sometimes and more than not, the church dressy appearance can be intimating to those we are trying to reach. I believe they will be more open to the gospel if evangelists or those doing the work of an evangelist could identify, empathize, and sympathize with the recipient.

The apostle Paul had the gift of volunteer poverty, but he was a well-off man. He was a Pharisee of the tribe of Benjamin, and his father was a Pharisee. He literally gave up his possessions to reach the poor. He traveled the known world of that time, spreading the gospel to the Gentiles.

First Corinthians 13:3, "And though I bestow all my goods to feed the poor."

I would say that he or she who has the gift of voluntary poverty also has the gift of giving. Because of this gift, this portion of the body of Christ can serve the Lord more effectively. They enjoy the sacrifice and have satisfaction in serving the Lord in this capacity. The newly converted at Pentecost sold all their goods to give to the poor, and they were glad to do so. God added to the church daily. Acts 2:44–47 says, "And all that believed were together, and had all things common; And sold their possessions and goods, and parted them to all men, as every man had need. And they, continuing daily with one accord in the temple, and breaking bread from house to house, did eat their meat with gladness and singleness of heart, Praising God, and having favour with all the people. And the Lord added to the church daily such as should be saved." Also compare this to Acts 4:34–37.

As Jesus went about, doing His ministry, He didn't have or carry a personal possession. He said to a scribe who wanted to follow Him, "Foxes have holes and the birds of the air have nests; but the Son of man hath not where to lay his head" (Matt. 8:20; also see Luke 9:58). Thus, throughout His ministry, Jesus went from house to house to stay. Often He stayed at the house of Mary, Martha, and Lazarus in Bethany. Jesus often went to have dinner at the houses of publicans and sinners, those who didn't have much in comparison to the church leaders of that time. Jesus was solely focused on His ministry and the will of His Father. Therefore, those who have the gift of voluntary poverty should focus on the task the Lord has given them. They shouldn't have a concern about material responsibility, but they should trust God for their daily bread.

Dream Interpretation

All people have dreams throughout their lives, whether they are believers or unbelievers, whether young or old. Often our dreams evolve around our current or past situations or relate to our future. Dreams and visions are important in our lives. Sometimes God gives us answers to our problems as well as warnings and directions.

Dreams are important ways for God to communicate His will to us. Most dreams have symbolic language and symbols. Not only do dreams relate to an individual, but one can also have dreams concerning others and nations. There are several people in the Bible who had dreams, visions, or both. Visions are on the same basis as dreams. Dreams come to those who are asleep, and visions come to those who are awake, perhaps in a trance. Here are a few Bible characters who had dreams and visions: Abimelech, Jacob, Pharaoh, Solomon, Nebuchadnezzar, Daniel, Joseph, Abram, Samuel, Joel, the wise men who sought Jesus, Ananias, Cornelius, Pilate's wife, the apostle Peter, and the apostle Paul. (Gen. 31:11; Gen. 41:4) (1 Sam. 3:15) (1 Kgs 3:5) (Matt. 1:20)

(Lk. 24:23) (Acts 9:10) (Acts 10:3) (Acts 18:9) (Rev. 9:17) (2 Cor. 12:1)

> After these things the word of the Lord came unto Abram in a vision, saying, Fear not, Abram: I am thy shield, and thy exceeding great reward. (Gen. 15:1)

> But God came to Abimelech in a dream by night, and said to him, Behold, thou art but a dead man, for the woman which thou hast taken; for she is a man's wife. (Gen. 20:3)

> He hath said, which heard the words of God, which saw the vision of the Almighty, falling into a trance, but having his eyes open. (Num. 24:4)

> In the first year of Belshazzar king of Babylon Daniel had a dream and visions of his head upon his bed: then he wrote the dream, and told the sum of the matters. (Dan. 7:1)

> And being warned of God in a dream that they should not return to Herod, they departed into their own country another way. (Matt. 2:12)

> When he was set down on the judgment seat, his wife sent unto him, saying, Have thou nothing to do with that just man: for I have suffered many things this day in a dream because of him. (Matt. 27:19)

> And it shall come to pass in the last days, saith God, I will pour out of my Spirit upon all flesh:

> and your sons and your daughters shall prophesy,
> and your young men shall see visions, and your old
> men shall dream dreams. (Acts 2:17)

> I was in the city of Joppa praying: and in a trance
> I saw a vision, A certain vessel descend, as it had
> been a great sheet, let down from heaven by four
> corners; and it came even to me. (Acts 11:5)

Some of the dreams we have are direct and clear, while others aren't so. The clear ones tend to bring immediate answers or results. Unclear dreams or visions tend to be symbolic in nature and futuristic. As we read and see the different dreams and visions, the symbols come from the dreamer's life and concerns. The books of Daniel, Psalms, Ezekiel, and Revelation are full of symbols. Therefore, the circumstances and heart of the dreamer dictate the type of symbols used in a dream or vision.

The undistinguishable dreams and visions need interpretation. This is why God has gifted some with the interpretation of dreams. A symbol in one person's dream or vision may not mean the same thing in another. There is no absolute symbol representation to equate all dreams and visions. The setting, environment, or circumstances of the dreamer have a vital role in interpretation. Nebuchadnezzar conquered the entire known world at that time. Within his pride, he was concerned about his kingdom, and he had a dream about it. It was Daniel and his three Hebrew friends who prayed about it, and God gave Daniel the interpretation of the dream (Dan. 2). When Daniel had dreams or visions, an angel or the angel Gabriel gave him the interpretation. When Joseph was in prison, Pharaoh's butler and baker had a dream, and Joseph gave the interpretation (Gen. 40).

The interpreter of the dream or vision must be candid in his or her presentation of the interpretation. We must remember that a dream's interpretation may not be as long as the dream itself, or the interpretation may be longer than the dream or vision. To have a good interpretation, the interpreter must get to the setting of the dreams or visions (for example, colors, numbers of people or things, and so forth). Not all interpretations bring good news, but all interpretations should increase one's faith and draw him or her nigh unto God. The dreamer or visionary will know inside whether the interpretation is true and from God. Dream interpretation comes from God. Joseph said to the baker and butler, "Do not interpretations belong to God?" Genesis 40:8 says, "And they said unto him, We have dreamed a dream, and there is no interpreter of it. And Joseph said unto them, Do not interpretations belong to God? tell me them, I pray you."

NOTES

CHAPTER 8
Ministry Gifts/Fivefold Ministry

———◇———

And he gave some, apostles; and some, prophets; and
some, evangelists; and some, pastors and teachers.
—Ephesians 4:11

These ministry gifts are given to those the Lord has called,
prepared, and ordained for the mission He has commanded to
the church. Many are called into the body of Christ, but few are
chosen for leadership or the fivefold ministry. Those who have
accepted the call into the ascension gift ministry should receive
and move at the command of the Lord. These ministries most
humble but bold in spirit for the work of the kingdom of God.
Through this effort and humble disposition, the Lord God will get
the glory in what we do.

There are some ministers who have gone the way of Balaam.
Woe unto them! There are some apostles, prophets, evangelists,
pastors, and teachers who are using their gifts for reward. Some are
asking for monetary gifts to speak over a believer's life. The term
used is "seed faith." The Lord thy God cannot be bribed; He saith
obedience is better than sacrifice. Some use their gift to obtain
prestige, applause, and even power. The minister should leave his
or her reward in the hands of the Lord. We must remember that
the pay isn't in the envelope.

The Lord was angry with Balaam, because he disobeyed God and sold his gift for profit. Balaam was a true prophet of God. Balak wanted Balaam to curse Israel because the Israelites outnumbered the Moabites. Balaam was eager to receive the reward of Balak the king of Moab. No matter whether the prophetic message was to curse or bless, Balaam wanted to be paid. The Lord God allowed Balaam not to curse Israel but to bless the nation instead. The result Balaam showed Balak was how he could corrupt the children of Israel (Num. 22–25). Second Peter 2:15–16 says, "Who have forsaken the right way, and are gone astray, following the way of Balaam, the son of Beor, who loved the wages of unrighteousness. But was rebuked for his iniquity; the dumb ass speaking with man's voice forbade the madness of the prophet."

The Office of the Apostle

And he gave some, apostles; and some, prophets; and
some evangelists; and some, pastors and teachers.
—Ephesians 4:11

Let us look at the office of the apostle. Who is an apostle? The word *apostle* is taken from the Greek word *apostolos*. Apostle or *apostolos* is defined as a "one sent forth[4]." An apostle is one who has been given a mission, who is an ambassador for Christ and has miraculous powers Christ gave to him or her. To some degree, the apostle can operate in all the ministry gifts. An apostle is one sent from Christ with a message and a mission. An apostle has a special message along with the gospel of Jesus Christ and the mission of establishing churches.

Some people have confined apostleship to its historical context. They contend that the only definition for an apostle is

---

[4] Vine's Complete Expository Dictionary of Old and New Testament Words, © 1984, 1996, Thomas Nelson, Inc. Nashville, TN

one who walked with Christ and witnessed His resurrection. But this is just one definition of an apostle. The apostles of Jesus Christ have died, but the office continues. Many people believe that when the apostles died, the ministry died with them, and the office of apostle ceased. But according to the word of God, we find that the ministry gift office of the apostle will remain intact until the maturing of saints and the coming of Christ. The characteristics of the apostolic ministry still exist. The Lord will send someone with a particular message and a unique mission. The message will reveal new truths of the word of God. The mission will be a nontraditional one.

A person whom the Lord has sent has been tested in his or her personal life and has experienced hard training. Many called into apostleship ministry will go through severe training before God commissions them. They will be judged by a higher standard than the layperson of the church will. Once a person acknowledges that the hard training is for the kingdom of God and for the ministry, he or she will embrace suffering. The apostle Paul expressed his hardship (2 Cor. 6:3–10). Through the effort to uphold the command of God to preach the gospel message and do the unique mission, often one who has been sent will experience opposition and much difficulty. In addition, the reason is that the devil won't allow a mission to go on without contesting it.

The first generation of apostles had to witness Jesus's ministry and be an eyewitness of His resurrection. The purpose and mission of these apostles were to proclaim Jesus Christ and introduce Him to the world. With the inspiration of the Holy Spirit and their eyewitness accounts, the apostles of Jesus Christ wrote the New Testament. Acts 1:15–22 says,

> And in those days Peter stood up in the midst
> of the disciples, and said, (the number of names
> together were about an hundred and twenty,) men
> and brethren, this scripture must needs have been

fulfilled, which the Holy Ghost by the mouth of David spake before concerning Judas, which was guide to them that took Jesus. For he was numbered with us, and had obtained part of this ministry. Now this man purchased a field with the reward of iniquity; and falling headlong, he burst asunder in the midst, and all his bowels gushed out. And it was known unto all dweller at Jerusalem; insomuch as that field is called in their proper tongue, Aceldama, that is to say, the field of blood. For it is written in the book Psalms, Let his habitation be desolate and let no man and dwell therein: and his bishopric let another take. Wherefore of these men which have companied with us all the time that the Lord Jesus went in and out among us, beginning from the baptism of John unto the same day that he was taken up from us, must one be ordained to be a witness with us of His resurrection.

Just before Pentecost, Peter and the other apostles chose another apostle to take Judas's place. The above text gives the qualifications. First, disciples had to be preachers or teachers of the word. Second, they had to be witnesses of Jesus's ministry. Third, they had to be witnesses of Jesus's resurrection. With their account of Jesus's ministry and resurrection, the first-generation apostles laid the foundation of the church. Therefore, there are no apostles related to the writing of the New Testament accounts.

The Holy Spirit will put the calling in the spirit of the called one. God's permissible will allows one to accept or reject the call. If one refuses to accept it, the Lord will start a process that makes one accept it. If the person continues to reject the call, the Lord will give the anointing and call to someone else. People cannot put others in the ministry, but they can confirm what God already put in their spirit.

The Holy Spirit will separate one to do the work of an apostle. We will find that the thought process of the apostle is different from all those around him or her, particularly laypeople. When we look at Paul and Barnabas's ministry, we see that they had been proclaiming the gospel for some time. At this point in their ministry, they were at the church in Antioch and were among other prophets and teachers. As they ministered to the Lord and fasted, the Holy Spirit said unto them to "separate [unto] me Barnabas and Saul for the work were unto I have called them." Acts 13:1–4 says,

> Now there were in the church that was at Antioch certain prophets and teachers; as Barnabas, and Simeon that was called a niger, and Lucius of Cyrene, and Manaen, which had been brought up with Herod the tetrarch, and Saul. As they ministered to the Lord, and fasted, the Holy Ghost said, the separate me Barnabas and Saul for the work where unto I have called them. And when they had fasted and prayed, and laid their hands on them, they sent them away. So they, being sent forth by the Holy Ghost, departed unto Seleucia; and from thence they sailed to Cyprus.

The Holy Spirit had called Paul and Barnabas before their commissioning at Antioch. We see that the Holy Spirit called them, which is in past tense. Therefore, Paul and Barnabas had the calling beforehand in their spirits. The prophets and teachers at Antioch confirmed their calling by the laying on of hands, and the Holy Spirit sent them forth. Matthew 10:1–4 says, "And when he had called unto him his twelve disciples, he gave them power against unclean spirits, to cast them out, and to heal all manner of sickness and all manner of disease. Now the names of the twelve apostles are these; The first, Simon, who is called Peter, and Andrew his brother; James the Son of Zebedee, and John his brother; Philip, and Bartholomew; Thomas, and Matthew the publican; James the son of Alphaeus, and Lebbaeus, whose surname was Thaddeus; Simon the Canaanite, Judas Iscariot, who also betrayed him."

We can see in Jesus's ministry that He called his disciples first to be fishers of men. He trained them and taught the word of God to them before He sent them out among the people. Through His examples and instructions, He prepared His disciples. The disciples weren't called apostles until after Jesus knew they were ready and had given them power to heal the sick and cast out demons. Jesus also warned His apostles of the persecution they would encounter for His name's sake (Matt. 10:22–23).

There were other apostles outside the original twelve. Some of the apostles who were with Jesus didn't write any books of the New Testament, but all of them ministered to others.

1. Andronicus (Rom. 16:7)
2. Apollos (1 Cor. 3:5)
3. Barnabas (Acts 14:4, 14)
4. Epaphroditus (Phil. 2:25)
5. James (Gal. 1:19)
6. Junias (Rom. 16:7)
7. Matthias (Acts 1:26)
8. Paul (Eph. 1:1)
9. Silas (1 Thess. 2:6)
10. Timothy (1 Tim. 1:18)
11. Titus (2 Cor. 8:23)
12. Two unnamed apostles (2 Cor. 8:18–22)
13. Seventy unnamed apostles Jesus Christ sent out (Luke 10:1)

Jesus Christ was the apostle of apostles. He was the only one who functioned in all the ministry gifts. He entrusted certain men with the fivefold ministry gifts to mature the saints of God.

CHAPTER 9
The Characteristics of an Apostle

Apostles will have power gifts imparted to them and be able to do signs, wonders, and mighty deeds through the Holy Spirit. They have the imparted power to cast out demons, heal the sick, and perform miracles. Signs are supernatural acts that appeal to the understanding. Wonders are supernatural power that appeals to the imagination. Power of supernatural origin and character that cannot be done by natural means generates miracles.

Apostles will vary in the gifts of the Holy Spirit and in the ministry gifts. Their primary gifts are working of miracles, gifts of healing, faith, word of wisdom, word of knowledge, discerning of spirits, and prophecy. Apostles and prophets, when ministering under the anointing, can reprove, correct, and give instructions in righteousness in the *rhema* word of Christ just like pastors and teachers give with the Holy Bible when they are preaching and teaching. The apostle prophesies or reveals the mind and counsel of God. When a believer operates in the gift of prophecy, he or she should edify, exhort, and comfort as defined in 1 Corinthians 14:3.

For one to serve in the office of the apostle, he or she must have a deep, personal experience and relationship with Christ. A true apostle won't proclaim to be an apostle, but the works of an apostle will speak for themselves. One can do the work of an apostle without claiming to be one. Humility is one of the characteristics of an apostle and other ministry offices. When one demonstrates the fruit of the Spirit, he or she will have a genuine concern and love for the body of Christ and not for any particular denomination. He or she will be others centered rather than self-centered. Apostles desire to see the body of Christ grow spiritually. They can equip the church for spiritual maturity and warfare. True apostles will labor to edify the whole body of Christ and glorify the Lord.

Apostles must have leadership abilities. Another word for *apostle* is *bishopric*. Apostles have a disposition of authority. They are overseers of a church or churches (Acts 1:20). Before the calling of an apostle, they must first learn discipleship and be faithful to their preaching or teaching ministry. Discipleship by definition is receiving into one's heart what he or she has learned and living by the principles of those teachings. Disciples are willing to follow leadership. To be a good leader, one must first learn how to follow. Before Jesus ordained His disciples to become apostles, they had to follow Jesus's leadership. Apostles have a spirit of boldness, not an arrogant spirit. They have boldness to stand up for what is right and for God and the gospel of Jesus Christ. Boldness needs to be present in the apostles' spirit to stand against the wiles of the devil and demonic forces.

A leader doesn't fall into cliques, go after unwise leadership, or follow the Joneses. Apostles have the natural ability to lead and set standards for others to follow as the Holy Spirit leads them. Apostles bring order and have organizational skills, along with the ability to establish churches and/or bring order to a church or churches. Apostles help to establish the truth of the word and the new moves of the Holy Spirit. They have an original thought process; that is to say, they don't think like others. The humility of apostles won't allow them to step out in the forefront on their own, but they will unintentionally be in the front. Others will look to them for leadership, and apostles will excel beyond their peers and have a sincere desire for others to mature as well.

An apostle must have spiritual wisdom. This wisdom isn't man's but God's. The apostle Paul often claimed to have the wisdom of the Spirit rather than that of man. Spiritual wisdom from God is unknown to man. An apostle can reveal spiritual truths with spiritual words, but they are all recognizable to those who believe and desire to hear from God. An apostle and any other of the ministry gift offices can function in both the spirit realm and natural realm. Note: The spirit realm (divine and satanic) recognizes the office of the apostle. God grants a person this supernatural wisdom for the purpose of building the church. Spiritual wisdom can be understood not in the flesh but in the spirit realm.

> Howbeit we speak wisdom among them that are perfect: yet not the wisdom of this world, nor all of the princes of this world, that come to nought: But we speak the wisdom of God in a mystery, even the hidden wisdom, which God ordained before the world unto our glory. (1 Cor. 2: 6–7)

> Now we have received, not the Spirit of the world, but the spirit which is of God; that we might know the things that are freely given to us of God. Which things also we speak, not in the words which man's wisdom teacheth, but which the Holy Ghost teacheth; comparing spiritual things with spiritual. (1 Cor. 2:12–13)

Apostles are the commanders of warfare. They can identify satanic spirits: familiar spirits, witchcraft, Jezebel spirits, and so forth. There are principalities and powers over cities and nations, and they are operating in some churches. There are strongholds that need to be torn down, and apostles have the anointing to do so. When strongholds are brought down, strength will come to people and the church.

When I was at a church in Houston, Texas, they led me to pray for the pastor for strength and deliverance. Praise the Lord, he was delivered. In the same church, there was a woman who needed a stronghold torn down. The Lord led me to pray for her; the strongholds in her life were torn down, and the woman was set free.

Faithfulness to God is necessary. An apostle and the other ministry gifts must be faithful to God and the work of the kingdom. God will reward faithfulness. If there is a higher calling on one's life, that person must prove his or her faithfulness where he or she is. Moreover, allow God to move in His plan and purpose, and develop you in His time and way. In the meantime, you can be faithful by building up the kingdom of God and through preparation.

We can prepare ourselves by studying the word of God and observing the movement of the Holy Spirit in the church. Faithfulness to God doesn't depend on what we say. If we never say a word, others can see faithfulness. Faithfulness isn't established over a short period. Sometimes establishing true faithfulness takes years. Faithfulness takes discipline and consistency. It means to be dependable and trustworthy all the time. You must be true to your word and in your walk. Your actions must be in harmony with what you say. First Corinthians 4:2 says, "Moreover, it is required in stewards, that a man be found faithful."

We must lay aside those insignificant things of this world that take up valuable time. The Lord must be first in our lives and have top priority. He is looking for those who will dedicate and consecrate themselves to Him and to the edification of the body of Christ. One should be totally committed to God. There shouldn't be any higher priority, love, or purpose than the purpose and will of the Lord.

We must discipline ourselves by studying the word of God, praying, and fasting. We should deny some things that will get in the way of the work of God. This doesn't always mean bad or evil things. Sometimes we can have too much of a good thing, and it will ultimately interfere with the work we must do for God. We can become too busy until we aren't accomplishing what the Lord wants us to do. Some of these things will have to be set aside for the Lord. Hebrews 12:1–2 says, "Wherefore seeing we also are compassed about with so great a cloud of witnesses, let us lay aside every weight, and sin which doth so easily beset us, and let us run with patience the race that is set before us, looking unto Jesus the author and finisher of our faith; who for the joy that was set before him endured the cross, despising the shame, and is set down at the right hand of the throne of God."

Because God has given us so much in giving us His only begotten Son, we should make time for Him and the ministry He has for us. If Jesus had to endure persecution and suffering on the cross for the church, so must the apostle and others of the fivefold ministry endure persecution and suffering for Jesus's sake. Suffering and persecution help one to minister to others. No one is exempt from trials and tribulations. We learn obedience and discipline through these acts of opposition. One is more inclined to read the word of God and pray more if opposition and unpleasant circumstances arise. Persecution should be embraced. The apostle understands that a crisis is often intended for the edification of the body of Christ and the glory of God. There are those who don't understand the move of God and lack the faith to grasp His vision and power. Matthew 5:11–12 says, "Blessed are ye, when men shall revile you, and persecute you, and shall say all manner of evil against you falsely, for my sake. Rejoice, and be exceeding glad: for great is your reward in heaven: for so persecuted they the prophets which were before you."

An apostle must have faith., which is written in the book of Hebrews. "Now faith is the substance of things hoped for, the evidence of things not seen" (Heb. 11:1). An apostle has the willingness to walk by faith and strive to live according to the word of God, carrying on with daily activities and trusting God in different situations that may arise. When we walk by faith, we must not try to be spiritual until we miss what the Lord is trying to show by means of the natural realm. A spiritual person can operate in both the spiritual and the natural realm. Apostles must believe and have faith in signs, wonders, and the miraculous powers of God. They must be willing to do just as the Lord has commanded them to do. The apostle doesn't second-guess what needs to be done; the person is sensitive to the leading of the Holy Spirit, lives by faith, and executes what the Lord has commanded.

Apostles have prophecy in their message and can operate in the prophetic ministry gift. The message will have revelations and directions. Not all messages are those of prosperity. They may give some revelations that deal with a person's personal life. They will bring about conviction in one's heart, repentance of sin, deliverance from any demonic spirit, healing for the sick, and hope for the despaired. The message will instruct, reprove, and give correction in righteousness. All prophetic messages will point back to the word of God in some form. Second Timothy 3:16–17 says, "All Scripture is given by the inspiration of God, and it is profitable for doctrine, for reproof, for correction, for instruction in righteousness: that the man of God may be perfect, thoroughly furnished unto all good works."

When Paul wrote this letter to Timothy, he encouraged Timothy to stand on the word of God. For Timothy to minister to the church effectively, he would have to preach and teach the word of God, regardless of the people's opinions. As we can see in this passage of scripture, not all messages are of health, wealth, and prosperity. Reproof is an act of reproving. The apostles' messages through the word of God find faults, misdeeds, and misconducts. They will also show us how to correct them and provide a word of hope and inspiration. Therefore, through these efforts, the saints of God can be nurtured and mature for the work of the kingdom, and sinners will be converted and saved.

Apostles must be apt to teach sound biblical doctrine. They

will have the training to understand the scriptures and will be able to teach so others will be able to understand. There are many doctrines in the world, but they will relate their teaching not on the topical basis but as it relates to the word of God. The word of God will generate their thoughts and inspirations. They will allow the scriptures to speak, and their thoughts will come from the word. Their preaching and teaching ministry will be founded on the word of God, not on their gifts. Even their signs and wonders will line up with the Holy Bible. All the fivefold ministers should be able to establish biblical doctrine, principles, and church doctrine (Acts 15:1–35).

Matthew 24:35 says, "Heaven and earth shall pass away, but my words shall not pass away." The church is founded on the word of God and the revelation of who Christ is. God will give revelations or reveal mysteries concerning His word, Christ, and the coming moves of the Holy Spirit. Upon Peter's spiritual recognition that Jesus was Christ, the Son of God, Jesus responded, "Upon this rock I will build my church (Matt. 16:18). God will give new revelations about His word and Christ, but some must grasp the old revelations that have been established in His word. Apostles will build their ministries based on the word of God rather than on their gifts. If a ministry is built on the gifts of apostles, then when apostles fall short of the glory of God or move on, the ministry itself will diminish. If it is built on the Holy Bible and the Holy Spirit, then it will stand.

Apostles can pull people together for God's plan. They will train them and motivate them according to the word of God, always speaking of the oneness of God and the unity of the church. They are builders of the kingdom. There are many people who claim to be apostles or are even gifted to receive revelations, but their positions and insights bring division among the body of Christ. Apostles, on the other hand, understand when Jesus said, "The harvest is plenty, but the laborers are few." Therefore, they will train others to evangelize the community and organized ministries.

Apostles train laypeople for the work of the kingdom, and

God will place ministers in the apostles' presence to be trained as leaders. Apostles can discern those who will be good leaders in the church. They will not only train ministers but also condition them for ordination. Apostles establish different kinds of ministries and set proved ministers over them. Apostles train and educate ministers on church government, structured sermon preparation and presentation, the move of the Holy Spirit in the church, and the move of God locally, nationally, and internationally. They can identify demonic, familiar spirits and the wiles of the devil.

Apostles will help other ministers identify with them and discover their position in God or spiritual growth. Apostles will recognize and help build up true ministers and won't tear them down because of a jealous spirit. They will encourage and strengthen them for the work. Apostles confirm the call God has set in a person's spirit pertaining to the fivefold ministry. Nowadays many pastors are intimidated by the ministers in their church and would rather hinder them than help them. The apostle Paul nurtured and trained his ministers, such as Timothy, Titus, Mark, Silas, and so forth.

Apostles know the law of impartation or how to activate the gift in the believer's life. *Impart* means "to grant or transfer."[5] Apostles have an apostolic anointing or a measure of grace in their lives. They have the supernatural ability to execute impartation so saints of God can fulfill their callings or destinies. They have the ability to perform the plan and purpose of God. Romans 1:11 says, "For I long to see you, that I may impart unto you some spiritual gift, to the end ye may be established."

Apostles should not only impart faith in the church through their preaching or teaching ministry but also be able to employ faith outside a church setting: at home or at a laundromat, a restaurant, work, or wherever they are. Through the law of impartation, apostles release other gifts to operate in the church. They receive

---

[5] The American Heritage Dictionary, Second College Edition © 1982, 1985 by Houghton Mifflin Company

revelations and impart them to the church so believers there may understand the move of God for the church. Before Jesus sent His disciples forth, He imparted to them part of His anointing so they would preach His word, cast out demons, heal the sick, and do miracles. Jesus empowered His disciples for the task to be done. Matthew 10:1 says, "And when he had called unto him his twelve disciples, he gave them power against unclean spirits, to cast them out, and to heal all manner of sickness and all manner of disease" (compare to Mark 6:7; Luke 9:1–2).

Jesus Christ, by the Holy Spirit, empowers apostles to impart graces unto the saints. When believers in the church operate in the gifts of the Holy Spirit or the fivefold ministry, they are called the "apostolic church." An apostolic church draws others into the kingdom of God. The flow of the anointing breaks yokes, brings healings, casts out demons, and brings miracles, deliverance, and blessings to those present. Isaiah 10:27 says, "And it shall come to pass in that day, that his burden shall be taken away from off thy shoulder, and his yoke from off thy neck, and the yoke shall be destroyed because of the anointing."

In every church, there are crises. The apostles know how to manage them. The apostle Paul always addressed the problems in the churches he had established. He had to address several issues in the Corinthians church, including the conduct of the church, division in the church, and the overall purpose of spiritual gifts. Therefore, apostles will enforce biblical standards of righteousness. They will confront immorality, false teachings, witchcraft, and any dysfunctions going on in the church. An apostolic anointing is needed to confront such situations. Galatians 2:11 says, "But when Peter was come to Antioch, I withstood him to the face, because he was to be blamed."

Types of Apostles

There are different types of apostles. Fivefold ministers will be able to operate under the anointing of the other ministries, but they

Dr. Brian E. W. Cretter

have a primary ministry. The following inserts Types of Apostles are from Dr. Bill Hamon's book *Apostles, Prophets, and the Coming Moves of God.*[6]

Apostolic Apostles: These are the apostles whose whole ministry expression is apostolic. These are the ones whose ministry expresses all the things apostles are capable of being and doing. The apostles will go to and fro, establishing churches. They will go about doing missionary work with signs, wonders, and miracles, but they will stay there only for a short period. They will establish works in spiritual truth and biblical doctrine.

Prophetic Apostles: These are true apostles who have a strong anointing for prophesying to individuals, churches, and nations. They can do this on their own or with a prophetic presbytery. In addition, the apostle Paul prophetically revealed the will of God and imparted spiritual graces and gifts. He laid hands on Timothy and prophesied his calling and gifts. First Timothy 4:14 says, "Neglect not the gift that is in thee, which was given thee by prophecy, with the laying on of the hands of the presbytery" (compare to 2 Tim. 1:6; Rom. 1:11).

Apostles will fulfill their ministry with discerning of spirits, having faith, and working of miracles. Apostolic prophets do similar things by their prophetic office gift of prophesying, the word of knowledge, and the gift of healing.

Evangelistic Apostles: These are more of the outreach ministers. Their hearts' desire is to evangelize the world, with more of the missionary ministry. They will have mass evangelism meetings. Their main message will be the plan salvation, but they also believe in the apostolic anointing. They believe in using signs, wonders, and the working of miracles to reach the hearts of the unsaved.

[6] Dr. Bill Hamon, Apostles, Prophets and the Coming Moves of God, Different Types of Apostles pages 223–227 (Destiny Image Publishers, Inc. Shippensburg, PA. 17257-0310, 1997), Reproduced by permission of Destiny Image Publishers, Inc.

Pastoral Apostles: The apostle James, the natural brother of Jesus, is an example of a pastoral apostle. The apostle James was a pastor at Jerusalem. James never conducted an apostolic crusade, but he wrote an epistle in the Bible. The other twelve apostles probably made apostle James their pastor. There was a situation when the apostles had to go to Jerusalem with a question concerning circumcising the Gentiles. The pastoral-apostle James gave them an answer and solutions to the issue at hand.

Teacher-Apostles: There are teacher-apostles teaching in Bible colleges, pastoring churches, and alternating between churches. They are concerned with proper doctrine and practical living. They would have an academy for kindergarten through twelfth grade, a Bible college, and training programs for the church. They would have volumes of outlines, teaching materials, and workbooks to help establish Christians in biblical truths and Christian experiences.

Regardless of what type of apostle minister one may be, God's supernatural power should be manifested in the apostolic ministry. With the example of these different kinds of apostles, this is a clear indication that one person cannot do it all. The apostles have been described as administrators of the church, those concerned about the church structure. Some of the authority must be delegated to true ministers who are also concerned about the church. Therefore, fivefold ministers can give themselves to more praying and studying the word of God so the apostolic anointing will manifest in miraculous ways and confirm the preached word of God.

NOTES

CHAPTER 10
The Office of the Prophet

And he gave some, apostles; and some, prophets and
some, evangelists, and some, pastors and teachers.
—Ephesians 4:11

The office of the prophet is a means by which the Lord Jesus
Christ communicates His will for an individual, church, or
nation. Are prophets needed in our modern time? Some who are
knowledgeable in the scriptures say we don't need prophets, that
they were only for Old Testament times. They suggest we have
God's will communicated to us in His word.

I suggest that God will speak to us whether it is by the Logos
or by a *rhema* word. All born-again believers have the Holy Spirit
dwelling on the inside, and God will talk to His children. However,
there are some whose faith isn't where it should be for them to
reach God. There are some who aren't saved and won't talk to
God. Therefore, God has some people He uses to forward His will
to them. In doing so, this means increases their faith in God, and
some come with a repentant heart.

If we limited the voice of God to the Holy Bible, there would
have been no need for prophets in the Old Testament. The
children of Israel had the Torah, the first five books of the Bible.
They had the instructions the Lord wanted them to have. There

were also messianic prophecies and concepts in the Torah. So, if they had the word of God, why did God use prophets in the Old Testament? As we view the New Testament, we must ask, why were there apostles and prophets? They had the word of God and the Word in the flesh, Jesus Christ. Prophets in the Old Testament and New Testament spoke forth the divine counsel of God to nations and individuals.

God ordained and set apart the office of the prophet. The call of God can come by way of dreams or visions, by prophecy, through Logos, or by a *rhema* word. A certain sign of any of the ministry gifts or any ministry is that burning desire God has put in one's spirit. You will find yourself doing it without trying to do so. The general basis of a call of an individual is that one must be faithful in worshipping God and have some idea of what the scriptures say.

The Greek word for prophet is *prophetes*. *Prophetes* means "one who speaks forth openly, a proclaimer of a divine message."[7] A prophet is one whom the Lord will speak through for the occasion at that moment. The given prophetic message can reveal things of the past, present, and future. The prophet declares what cannot be known by natural means. The main objective for the prophet and prophesying is to draw people closer to God and so they will believe in Him. Deuteronomy 18:18 says, "I will raise them up a prophet from among their brethren, like unto thee, and will put my word in his mouth; and he shall speak unto them all that I shall command him."

The word of a prophet comes directly from God. The prophet under the anointing speaks on behalf of the Lord. Old Testament prophets spoke the mind of God. New Testament prophets speak the mind of Christ as well. The message of the prophet isn't always good news, although we see that so many people are looking for

---

[7] Vine's expository dictionary of new testament word, unbridged edition, MacDonald Publishing Company Mclean, VA, 22101

this type of message. Sometimes it will bring forth convictions, rebuke, instructions, and confirmation. Whether the word from the prophet is good or bad, it should draw one closer to God.

When we compare the gift of prophecy to the office of the prophet, we see that one who has been called to the office of the prophet can bring words of conviction, rebuke, and instruction, whereas one who has the gift of prophecy is limited to exhortation, comfort, and edification. All believers are subject to the gift of prophecy. When one is inspired to give a testimony and tell what God had done for him or her and give words of encouragement, that is a form of prophecy. First Corinthians 14:31 says, "For ye all prophesy one by one, that all may learn, and all may be comforted."

The children of Israel weren't a born-again people. Their spirits weren't regenerated, so God couldn't deal with them on an individual basis in the spirit. He couldn't witness to their inner person because the inner person wasn't quickened. The kings, priests, and prophets were the only ones anointed for their tasks. The prophet was the only person anointed to bring forth the word of God to His people. The kings were anointed to rule over the people. The priests were those who taught and exhorted the people with the laws of God. They also carried out the sacrificial ceremonies. If any of the kings or priests were concerned about a situation and desired to hear a word from God, they sought out the prophet.

Second Kings 3:11 says, "But Jehoshaphat said, 'Is there not here a prophet of the Lord, that we may inquire of the Lord by him?' And one of the king of Israel's servants answered and said, here is Elisha, of Shaphat, who poured water on the hands of Elijah." King Jehoshaphat wanted to know the outcome of the war they were about to enter with the Moabites. Elisha went before the Lord God and prophesied that Israel would be victorious in their campaign against the Moabites.

The prophet should be able to prophesy and proclaim or explain the word of God. He is a preacher or teacher of the Holy

Bible or both. The first priority of the Old and New Testament prophet was to preach or teach the word of God. If you remember, the Old Testament prophets always preached repentance to the nation of Israel. The prophets Elijah and Elisha were teachers of the word of God. They taught and trained other prophets, who were called the sons of the prophets. Second Kings 4:38 says, "And Elisha came again to Gilgal: and there was a dearth in the land; and the sons of the prophets were sitting before him."

The prophet Isaiah was both a preacher and a teacher of the scriptures. Isaiah had prophecy contained in his preaching, and he frequently used the phrases "Fear not", "I have chosen you", "redeemed you", "I called you by name", "you are mine" (Isa. 41:10f; 43:1; 44:1). The most profound and renowned prophetic preaching of Isaiah is in chapter 7:14 and Isaiah 53. "Therefore the Lord himself shall give you a sign; Behold, a virgin shall conceive, and bear a son, and shall call his name Immanuel", Isa. 7:14

In Isaiah 28:23, Isaiah was a teacher of wisdom and the law, and he taught his disciples. Isaiah 8:16 says, "Bind up the testimony; seal the law among my disciples."

The subject matter determines the content of the prophet's message. Most prophets have their own form of prophesying. Sometimes one who serves in the office of the prophet, while teaching or preaching, may have a message at the spur of the moment that may not fit the context of the prepared message. Both Old and the New Testament prophets were anointed with the word of knowledge and the word of wisdom.

Although the apostle Paul was an apostle, prophet, teacher, and preacher, he presented himself as a preacher before any of the other offices he held. Second Timothy 1:11 says, "Whereunto I am appointed a preacher, and an apostle, and a teacher of the gentiles."

Jesus Christ was a preacher before He prophesied. His initial ministry was preaching. When Jesus met the Samaritan woman at Jacob's well, He used the surroundings to preach the word of God.

Then He prophesied to her to draw her into the area of worship and belief in Him. Luke 4:18–19 says, "The Spirit of the Lord is upon me, because he hath anointed me to preach the gospel to the poor; he hath sent me to heal the brokenhearted, to preach deliverance to the captives, and recovering of sight to the blind, to set at liberty them that are bruised, to preach the acceptable year of the Lord."

The Old Testament prophets of Israel were summoned to speak on behalf of the Lord God of Israel. The prophets spoke just what they had heard from the Lord. Often the Lord God spoke to the prophets by way of visions and dreams. The prophets were the only ones who could speak for the Lord. Not all prophets present their message in the same way. There are different methods God uses to get what He wants to say across to His people.

We see the phrases often used—"The Lord had said or "Thus saith the Lord." The word of the prophet always aligned with the word of God. There were some like Jeremiah who were straightforward and direct with their prophetic messages. Ezekiel was dramatic with his messages. Prophecy ultimately employs the messenger formula as the most direct means of expressing its function. The prophecy and instructions the Lord gives dictate the way they are said and presented. The words "Thus saith the Lord" introduce the messenger formula. The prophets used these words with the understanding of their roles as ambassadors for the Lord.

The prophets prophesied in the form in which the word was given to them, which was in the first person. They didn't allow themselves to add or take away from what God had given them, but they spoke as if they were the Master themselves. The Lord God gave a word to Elijah to give to Ahab for the evil he had done. First Kings 21:19 says, "And thou shalt speak unto him, saying, Thus saith the Lord, Hast thou killed, and also taken possession? And thou shalt speak unto him, saying, Thus saith the Lord, In the place where dogs licked the blood of Naboth shall dogs lick thy blood, even thine."

The Lord gave the prophet Jeremiah a word of reproof for the nation of Israel. Jeremiah spoke it just as if the Lord Himself had. Jeremiah 2:5 says, "Thus saith the Lord, What iniquity have your fathers found in me, that they are gone far from me, and have walked after vanity, and are become vain?"

The prophet always gave some form of prefix before introducing the message. The prefix was used to draw attention to the message. In the case of divine warnings, there was a diatribe, a denunciation. For a promise, the prophet would give an exhortation. The prophet always separated the prefix from the message. The diatribe or exhortation introduced the message, but the message was a direct word from God at the moment of inspiration.

Old Testament and New Testament prophets didn't operate in the office of the prophet all the time. They functioned only as God or the Holy Spirit led them. Many look for prophets to prophesy every time they see them. Then there are some prophets who, because of this notion, try to operate without the anointing. Often this leads to reliance on the flesh rather than on the Spirit. First Corinthians 12:11 says, "But all these worketh that one and the selfsame Spirit, dividing to every man severally as he will."

The Characteristics of the Prophet

Prophets must be sensitive to the voice of the Lord. They do this through much prayer and meditation on the word of God. There are other voices that come into the spirit realm. Not every voice we hear is the voice of the Lord. Some who aren't spiritually mature mistake the other voices for the voice of the Holy Spirit. Believers must acknowledge that Satan is a spirit. He has demonic angels and evil spirits in operation. First Corinthians 14:10 says, "There are, it may be, so many kinds of voices in the world, and none of them is without signification."

If people know of a situation or desire to hear something from the Lord, they will entertain a thought for so long until they believe their own voices to be the voice of God and say, "Thus saith the Lord." If they don't know for sure what the Lord's voice sounds like, then it's best not to say or do anything until they know for sure when the Spirit is speaking. The voice of the Lord will edify the church and glorify God. Other voices exalt themselves rather than God. Some people sincerely desire to know the voice of God, because they yield themselves to a familiar spirit; this doesn't mean they have a demonic spirit. However, it suggests they need to discern the difference between the two spirits.

The Lord teaches us His voice as we study His word and through prayer and meditation. He will also teach us His voice as we go through different crises in our lives. When we experience a crisis, often it brings about a more disciplined disposition. We tend to read the Bible more and pray more sincerely. The difficult situations that occur in our lives often lead us to draw nigh unto God.

The Holy Spirit won't speak of Himself, but He will speak of what the Lord Jesus Christ has told Him and shown Him. Therefore, the voice of the Lord is that still, tender, masculine voice that speaks deep down on the inside. He speaks and bears witness with our spirits. He also speaks with a voice of authority. Jesus refers to the Holy Spirit in the masculine gender. He always addresses the Holy Spirit as "He." The voice of God conveys from our spirit person to our soul or psyche in what makes it identifiable to the believer. He speaks messages or thoughts to us that aren't our normal train of thought.

> Howbeit when he, the Spirit of truth, is come, he will guide you into all truth: for he shall not speak of himself; but whatsoever he shall hear, that shall he speak: and he will show you things to come. (John 16:13)

> The Spirit itself beareth witness with our spirit, that we are the children of God. (Rom. 8:16)

No one should put all his or her trust in prophecy. The Holy Spirit leads New Testament believers on the inside with their inner witness. Most prophecy confirms what God had already put in one's spirit. Every now and then, God gives a new revelation to someone, but then, as with all prophecy, it must be proved by the word of God. The inner witness is that peaceful or disturbing feeling we get when we are faced with a situation.

Prophets must be able to discern the difference among angelic spirits, demonic spirits, and human spirits. One can follow prophets and have some other kind of spirit other than the Holy Spirit. Not every one who says, "Praise the Lord" or makes a proclamation is of the Lord. The apostle Paul met a woman of such. This young girl had a spirit of divination (foretelling of future events). She was a fortune-teller who followed Paul and others as they went to pray. She did this for several days. She kept shouting, "These men are the servants of the most high God, which show us the way of salvation." The apostle Paul was grieved and rebuked that spirit (Acts 16:16–18).

Demonic spirits will use the word of God. They will take scriptures out of the Holy Bible and make them mean something other than what God intended. If you remember, Satan deceived Eve with the word of God. He tried to tempt Jesus with the word of God. Evil spirits will always make a presentation that will lead to the realm of the flesh and self-glorification. That is why the prophet should know the word of God and be able to discern spirits. If the prophet receives a word that may cause confusion, then it ought not to be uttered. Some saved people allow the devil to use them. Some speak forth division rather than unity. Some speak forth cursing rather than blessing. God isn't the author of confusion. First John 4:1 says, "Beloved, believe not every spirit, but try the spirits whether they are of God: because many false prophets are gone out into the world."

Those who are in the office of the prophet can forthtell and foretell. Forthtelling is preaching or teaching the word of God by inspired preparation and presentation. Foretelling (revealing future events) comes only by the word of wisdom as the Holy Spirit wills. In the Old Testament, prophets mostly foretold future events. They prophesied judgment on Israel and gave many prophecies of Jesus Christ coming as the messiah.

As with the entire fivefold minister, prophets would gather their thoughts from the scriptures. Some prophecies come from a passage of scripture. Prophets will allow the scriptures to dictate to them what to say in preaching and teaching God's word. The object of preaching is giving the scriptures a voice and bringing them to life. We have many ministers who have thoughts on a subject, and they find passages of scripture to fit their ideas. The church today has a desire to hear what the word of God has to say rather than one's ideas about the scriptures.

Prophetic preaching or teaching is extemporaneous. It is revelation knowledge given by the inspiration of God. The prophetic word that comes is impulsive and inspirational out of the normal path of the preaching and teaching. Prophetic preaching and teaching from the Bible convey the direct voice of God. First Peter 4:11 says, "If any man speak, *let him speak* as the oracles of God; if any man minister, *let him do it* as of the ability which God giveth: that God in all things may be glorified through Jesus Christ, to whom be praise and dominion for ever and ever Amen" (emphasis added).

Although prophets have a prepared message, their minds and spirits must be open to divine intervention in the presentation. Through the prophet's willingness to be open in the presentation, the Holy Spirit will give something spontaneously to meet the needs of a person or people. The preaching and teaching of apostles and prophets always build up the saints of God. The Christian who desires to grow will appreciate the message given, but on the other hand, those who refuse to mature will think the message given is harsh. The message of the apostle and prophet will speak to the spirit rather than to the flesh. A prophet is a good storyteller. With what prophets see, feel, and hear in the scriptures, they can paint a picture for others to see.

He must know the word of God to bring forth a *rhema* word from the Logos. The Bible reveals the mind and will of God, His plans and purposes, and His decrees and principles. The word of God measures all expressions, standards, concepts, revelations, and prophecies. The word of God is perfect, and it is God's communication in written form. Any prophecies given must conform to the Holy Bible. Second Timothy 3:16–17 says, "All scripture is given by inspiration of God, and is profitable for doctrine, for reproof, for correction, for instruction in righteousness: That the man of God may be perfect, throughly furnished unto all good works."

Rhema is a Greek word meaning a selective word from the word of God for an individual, a company of people, or a nation. *Rhema* denotes what is spoken or uttered in speech and writing: in the singular, or a word.[8] A *rhema* word isn't in reference to the whole Bible, but it is a portion of scripture or a spoken illustration of the scriptures that the Holy Spirit brings to our remembrance for a specific occasion and need. This singular spoken word must be received by faith. When a *rhema* word is received, it will bring encouragement and build faith, power, and fulfillment in the life of the believer. Romans 10:17 says, "So then faith cometh by hearing, and hearing by the word of God."

Therefore, the Logos pertains to the Holy Bible as a whole, whereas a *rhema* word consists of a singular scripture or story from the Logos. The foundation of a *rhema* word is the Logos. The work of the Holy Spirit can bring a personal *rhema* to an individual for conviction, encouragement, and comfort. If you are reading the word of God, the Holy Spirit can enlighten the meaning of a story or scripture being read. The still, small voice of the Holy

---

[8] W. E. Vine's Expository Dictionary of the New Testament Words, Macdonald, p. 1253, Macdonald Publishing Company Mclean, Virginia 22101

Spirit will give birth to a *rhema* in your spirit. The Holy Spirit will impress a word in your soul. It is a quick thought or idea from God, which has not been meditated on. The inner man and the Holy Spirit always ensure a *rhema* word. A *rhema* word is directly from God, but a personal prophecy is from one person to another. All prophecies should line up with the word of God and confirm the inner witness.

Prophecy is a divine word spoken forth for edification, exhortation, and comfort through the revelation gifts: the gift of knowledge, the gift of wisdom, and the discerning of spirits. All these can be in one prophetic message, or one or the other can be manifested. Prophecy will always be in part. The prophet may give the big picture with some details but not precept upon precept. The prophet is used more consistently in these areas than in the other fivefold ministers.

The word of knowledge is a fact known only between the recipient and God. It is a fact that has to do with the past or present. It is a supernatural word that reveals a condition or state of a believer or nonbeliever that couldn't have been known by natural means. It is God's knowledge. God gives the prophet a word of knowledge to bring one closer to God. In some cases, the word of knowledge brings one into the realm of salvation and can come by way of dreams and visions.

Elisha was given a word of knowledge concerning his servant Gehazi. Elisha turned down the pay Naaman was going to give him, but his servant Gehazi went after Naaman for his own selfish gain. Elisha observed the exchange between Gehazi and Naaman. Second Kings 5:26 says, "And he said unto him, Went not mine heart with thee, when the man turned again from his chariot to meet thee? Is it a time to receive money, and to receive garments, and olive-yards, and vineyards and sheep, and oxen, and menservants, and maidservants?"

A word of knowledge came to Jesus when He ministered to the woman at the well. John 4:18 says, "For thou hast had five husbands; and he whom thou now hast is not thy husband: in that saidst thou truly."

By the word of knowledge, the prophet is shown the situation or condition of the person being ministered to. The prophet or the one who has the gift of the word of knowledge may receive just one word or many. If prophets receive one word, then they must step out on faith with the one word, and God will provide the rest of the word.

God can give a word of knowledge dealing with warning or judgment. Often when a word is given for judgment or warning, it is given in a private setting. Prayerfully the prophet will always use wisdom when there is a public word given to an individual. God isn't out to embarrass anyone. When mature prophets have a word for the church, they consult with the pastor first. If the pastor gives consent, they will give a general word to the church.

The prophet Nathan gave King David a word of knowledge for his sinful deed. David had committed adultery in secret, but the Lord had seen him and sent the prophet Nathan to David (2 Sam. 12:1-14).

The word of wisdom is a supernatural word given for the future. God gives prophets the true nature of situations and conditions. Therefore, when they speak a word of wisdom, they speak about things that will come to pass. Often the word of wisdom is given in a public forum. This wisdom is from God and isn't of man. This is where most of the problems occur for prophets and the church. Some people just want to hear prophets give a word of wisdom for them. Some prophets try to operate in the prophetic word of wisdom just because they were asked to. Prophets who try to operate without the anointing put forth a dangerous disposition. The office of the prophet deals with the souls of the people. If prophets give a word that wasn't given by divine inspiration, they can hinder the faith of the believer. Both the word of knowledge and the word of wisdom should bear witness with the spirit of the recipient.

In Acts 11:28, we find a word of wisdom the prophet Agabus gave on a universal level. "And there stood up one of them named Agabus, and signified by the Spirit that there should be great dearth thoughout all the world: which came to pass in the days of Claudius Caesar."

Agabus gave the apostle Paul a word of wisdom concerning his journey to Jerusalem (Acts 21:10–11). Agabus prophesied what was going to happen, but he didn't tell Paul what to do. He didn't try to guide or direct the apostle Paul.

The word of wisdom is God allowing us to know what will happen in the future to help prepare us for what is to come. Therefore, when that time comes, we can exercise our faith and trust God in our situations.

When prophets give a warning, it will be up to recipients to change their behavior and adjust the results of the warning. When prophets pronounce judgment, it is too late to change its course because heaven has decreed it. Old Testament prophets prophesied with the word of wisdom. There are some in the New Testament who prophesied with the word of wisdom. The Lord gave the apostle Paul a word of wisdom concerning his ministry. Acts 23:11 says, "And the night following the Lord stood by him, and said, Be of good cheer, Paul: for as thou hast testified of me in Jerusalem, so must thou bear witness also at Rome."

The apostle Paul was under attack from the Pharisees and Sadducees. They threatened to persecute him for taking a stand for Christ and tried to hinder the apostle from doing a work for Jesus Christ. However, the Lord sent the apostle Paul a reassuring word of wisdom. He must go and witness in Rome.

In 1 Kings 17:1, Elijah declared to King Ahab, the king of Israel, that it wouldn't rain in Israel for three years. The Lord gave King Ahab a word of wisdom through the prophet Elijah. First King 17:1 says, "And Elijah the Tishbite, who Gilead, said unto Ahab, As the Lord God of Israel liveth, before whom I stand, there shall not be dew nor rain these years, but according to my word."

Samuel gave the children of Israel a word of wisdom. They were determined to have a king like all the other nations. They refused to continue to have the Lord reigning over them through the prophet Samuel. Samuel was grieved, but the Lord told him, "They have not rejected thee, but they have rejected me, that I should not reign over them." The Lord told Samuel to tell the people what the outcome would be if they wanted a king. This word of wisdom wasn't good news. The people heard not the words of the prophet and insisted on having a king. The Lord allowed it to be so. The king Samuel prophesied about was an abusive king. This king was Saul (1 Sam. 8:1–22).

Judges 4 calls Deborah a prophetess. She was in a leadership position, a judge of Israel. The Lord spoke through her to Barak. Deborah, the prophetess, gave Barak a prophetic word concerning the war with Jabin's army. She gave a word of knowledge dealing with the command God gave Barak to go against Jabin's army and a word of wisdom, telling him what the outcome of the war would be. Judges 4:4 says, "And Deborah, a prophetess, the wife of Lapidoth, judged Israel at that time."

Deborah was a woman of God. The Spirit of the Lord came upon the judges in Israel that they may deliver them out of the hands of their enemies (Judg. 3:16).

Huldah, who dwelt in Jerusalem, was a prophetess (2 Kings 22:14–20). She knew the word of God and prophesied according to the situation at hand. The king of Judah at that time was Josiah. He sent messengers to the prophetess to receive a word from God. Through the word of wisdom, she pronounced judgment against Israel, and she said King Josiah would die in peace.

The New Testament considered Anna a prophetess. She was a widow for eighty-four years and spent all her time in the temple, praying and fasting. She meditated on the word of God night and day, and she devoted her life to God just as the scriptures say widows and single women should do. Through her devotion to God, the Lord used her in the prophetic realm (Luke 2:36–38).

Miriam, the sister of Aaron, was a prophetess. She was a prophet over the music ministry and spoke prophetically through songs. She conducted and led the praise after God delivered Israel at the crossing of the Red Sea. Exodus 15:20 says, "And Miriam the prophetess, the sister of Aaron, took a timbrel in her hand; and all the women went out after her with timbrels and with dances."

Music enhances the prophetic ministry. Many churches and musician are missing the important role music has in the spirit realm. Music ministers to the souls of believers and induces worshippers to surrender themselves to the unction of the Holy Spirit. The minister of music should pray before selecting songs for the worship service. Every musician should be able to recognize the work of the Holy Spirit. There are times when the musician should play worship music. Then there are other times when the anointing of the Holy Spirit calls for music of praise.

> When an evil spirit came upon King Saul, David played the harp for him until the spirit left the presence of Saul. Saul disobeyed the Lord. The Lord withdrew his anointing from Saul. Saul's servant suggested to him that he should summon David, the son of Jesse, to play the harp for him. David was well skilled in playing the harp. (1 Sam. 16:14–22)

> And it came to pass, when the evil spirit from God was upon Saul, that David took an harp, and played with his hand; so Saul was refreshed, and was well, and the evil spirit departed from him. (1 Sam. 16:23)

The sounds of the harp usher in a soothing, worshipful kind of atmosphere. When the Holy Spirit presents Himself through worship, the musicians, particularly the organist, should play worshipful types of music. When the Holy Spirit calls for music of praise, the minister of music should bring about minstrels of praise.

Elisha prophesied for Jehoshaphat because he wanted to know what would be the outcome of a war with the Moabites. He inquired whether there was a prophet of the Lord that he may ask of the Lord concerning the matter. One of Jehoshaphat's servants suggested that he should go and see Elisha. Before Elisha could prophesy to the king, he asked for a minstrel. While the minstrel was playing, Elisha prophesied instruction and victory for King Jehoshaphat. Second Kings 3:14–15 says, "And Elisha said, As the Lord of hosts liveth, before whom I stand, surely, were it not that I regard the presence of Jehoshaphat, the king of Judah, I would not look toward thee, nor see thee. But now bring me a minstrel. And it came to pass, when the minstrel played, that the hand of the Lord came upon him."

David had a music ministry that was instrumental in the prophetic ministry. He had 288 people in his music ministry. First Chronicles 25:1, 7 says, "Moreover, David and the captains of the host separated to the service of the sons of Asaph, and of Heman, and of Jeduthun, who should prophesy with harps, with psalteries, and with cymbals … So the number of them, with their brethren who were instructed in the songs of the Lord, even all that were cunning, was two hundred fourscore and eight."

Prophets can see into the spirit realm and therefore should be able to discern spirits. Those prophets who have the gift of discerning spirits know whether a spirit is good or evil. As we have discovered, not everything prophets see or hear in the spirit realm is of God. If prophets cannot discern spirits and listen to the wrong spirits, they will bring confusion and destruction to a church. First Corinthians 14:10 says, "There are, it may be, so many kinds of voices in the world, and none of them is without signification."

The one who serves in the office of the prophet must know the difference between the spirits. The gift of the word of knowledge often operates with the gift of discerning spirits. Most people stay away from this area when it comes to prophets. Some suppose prophets will uncover their wrongdoing. Mature prophets will tell one in private whether that is the case. The Lord will show prophets the motives of the spirits and their origin. The spirit or spirits someone has motivate him or her.

Acts 19:13–16 says, "Then certain of the vagabond Jews, exorcist, took upon them to call over them which had evil spirits, saying, We adjure you by Jesus whom Paul preacheth. And there were seven sons of one Sceva, a Jew, and chief of the priest, which did so. And the evil spirit answered and said, Jesus I know, and Paul I know; but who are ye? And the man in whom the evil spirit was leaped on them, and overcame them, and prevailed against them, so that they fled out of that house naked and wounded."

In this account, a man possessed with evil spirits attacked seven men of the Jewish faith. However, these men tried to cast out devils, something they were unauthorized to do. The spirits in the man caused him to attack these men.

In Mark 5, a man in the graveyard was yelling and cutting his body with stones. No man could bind or control him. This man had a legion of demons in him, but he met Jesus. Jesus cast out six thousand spirits from this man. The spirits within him caused him to abuse his body.

The Lord supernaturally shows prophets the inner being or heart of an individual. The Lord will show this to prophets so they can be delivered or healed of the spirits controlling them.

Some sicknesses or diseases are demonically driven. Satan attacks the minds and bodies of individuals. Often the spirit or spirits that have afflicted someone will manifest what kind of spirit they are. They will come through the voice or actions of the person. If there isn't a manifestation of an unclean spirit, the Lord will put it in the spirit of a prophet if there is a prophet present.

Jesus healed a man's lunatic son (Matt. 17:14–21; Mark 9:14–29). The disciples couldn't do it because they lacked faith. The father confronted Jesus and told Him about his son's illness. The epileptic spirit this son had caused him to be troubled, harm his body, gnash his teeth, and foam at the mouth. Jesus cast out the spirit by saying, "Thou dumb and deaf spirit, I charge thee, come out of him, and enter no more into him" (Matt. 17:18; Mark 9:25).

A subtle case of a manipulating spirit was when the sorcerer Simon heard Philip preach the word of God. Simon believed, and Philip baptized him. In Jerusalem, word came that Philip had preached and many believed, but they weren't filled with the Holy Spirit. The apostles sent Peter and John to Samaria to lay hands on the new converts. When the apostles laid hands on the believers, they were filled with the Holy Spirit. When Simon saw the Holy Spirit involved in the life of the newly converted people, he desired to purchase the Holy Spirit.

Peter discerned Simon's spirit and rebuked him for his sins. Simon wanted to purchase the Holy Spirit so he could manipulate the people for profit. Simon's outward expression to purchase the power of the Holy Spirit was one sin. The second sin was an inner manipulating spirit for profit. Through the Holy Spirit, Peter discerned the spirit within Simon (Acts 8:18–25).

Prophets can operate within the realm of signs, wonders, and works of miracles. Through the gift of the word of knowledge, God reveals sicknesses and diseases to them. There were many occasions when the Lord wrought miracles by the hands of Paul. Acts 3:3 says, "Long time therefore abode they speaking boldly in the Lord, which gave testimony unto the word of his grace, and granted signs and wonders to be done by their hands."

In the city of Iconium, Paul preached the word of God, and the Lord did miracles by the hands of Paul and Barnabas. Notice the sequence: (1) Paul preached the gospel, and then (2) the faith induced in the recipients led to their receiving healings of the Lord. Acts 14:8–10 says, "And there sat a certain man at Lystra, impotent in his feet, being a cripple from his mother's womb, who never had walked: The same heard Paul speak: who stedfastly beholding him, and perceiving that he had faith to be healed, said with a loud voice, stand upright on thy feet. And he leaped and walked."

After Paul preached the word of God, he saw there was a man lame from birth. Paul perceived or saw the man had faith to be healed and commanded the man to stand. The man leaped from his lame position and began to walk.

Elisha the prophet raised the son of a Shunammite woman. This woman's womb was closed, and he prophesied that she would have a son. A year later, the woman had a son. But as the son grew older, he became sick and died in his mother's arms. She summoned Elisha. Elisha prayed and did as the Lord commanded. The son rose from his lifeless position and began to breathe (2 Kings 4:19–37).

Prophets may operate within the realm of the miraculous, but their primary task is to prophesy the mind and will of God for the body of Christ, nations, or individuals. The position of prophets is to restore or enhance the faith of believers. Through prophets, God confirms His word and strengthens the faith of believers.

NOTES

CHAPTER 11
The Office of the Evangelist

And he gave some, apostles; and some, prophets, and
some, evangelists, and some pastors, and teachers.
—Ephesians 4:11

First, let us define the word *evangelist*. The Greek word for *evangelist*
is *euaggelistes*, denoting a messenger of good news. The one God
ordains to the office of the evangelist is a proclaimer of the gospel.
Because a person spreads the gospel, that doesn't make him or her
an evangelist. When a person becomes well versed in the scriptures,
that doesn't make him or her an evangelist. There is a difference
between the office of the evangelist and the work of evangelism.

Euaggelion is the Greek work for good news or the gospel.
It stresses the salvation message: the death, burial, resurrection,
and ascension of our Lord and Savior Jesus Christ. It is the
responsibility of all born-again believers to proclaim the gospel of
the kingdom of God. Jesus commissioned all His disciples to spread
the gospel throughout the world. Mark 16:15–16 says, "And he said
unto them, go ye into all the world, and preach the gospel to every
creature. He that believeth and is baptized shall be saved: but he
that believeth not shall be damned."

A person can do the work of an evangelist by spreading the
salvation message. We are saved by grace through faith in Christ

Jesus. The true story we all should be spreading is that Jesus died for our sins and on the third day rose from the grave.

As the apostle Paul wrote to the Corinthians about spreading the gospel of Jesus Christ through the ministry of reconciliation, all believers have the same ministry. As we go, the proclamation of the word of salvation should be given to all men. Second Corinthians 5:18 says, "And all things are of God, who hath reconciled us to himself by Jesus Christ, and hath given to us the ministry of reconciliation."

The purpose of the work of evangelism is to bring the awareness of God to the lost. The main focus is God and what He has done for us through His Son, Jesus Christ.

Evangelism can take on many forms. It can come through books, music, poems or psalms, the testimonies of the saints, exhortations, and the principles of preaching and teaching the word of God.

The evangelist in Ephesians 4:11 is a position Jesus Christ called and established. As we discovered, fivefold ministers are leaders and not laypersons. They are primarily preachers or teachers of the word of God. The one in the office of the evangelist must know and understand the word of God. To know different scriptures isn't enough. One must know *and* understand the scriptures to properly apply them to an individual's life. An evangelist isn't an apostle, although an apostle can operate in the office of the evangelist.

The Characteristics of an Evangelist

Evangelists have compassion for the lost souls of the world. The evangelists' desire is to win souls for Christ. Their heart is the heart of God concerning salvation for the world. John 3:16–17 says, "For God so loved the world, that he gave his only begotten Son, that whosoever believeth in him should not perish, but have everlasting life. For God sent not his Son into the world to condemn the world; but that the world through him might be saved."

Evangelists function as if nothing matters outside the plan of salvation. They have little concern when it comes to the gifts of the Holy Spirit or other ministry gifts or fivefold ministry. Presently, we have many who call themselves evangelists and place emphasis on their position. True evangelists aren't concerned about a position. Their main concern is seeking those who are lost.

Evangelists have the gift of exhortation. They have the gift to urge people to come to the Lord and be saved. They don't write anybody off as having no hope. They introduce hope to the hopeless. Evangelists look beyond a person's faults and see what he or she can be through Jesus Christ.

The office of the evangelist is a roving ministry. Evangelists look to go where the sinners are. They plant the seed of the word of God in the community. They cannot make full proof of their ministry by staying at the altar. Their desire and passion are to go out and win souls for the Lord. Evangelists should be sensitive to the voice of the Holy Spirit. When they open to the Holy Spirit, they will receive directions regarding where they should go. They may want to go in one direction, but the Lord may want them to go in another one. Once evangelists reach their destination, the Lord will tell them whom to evangelize. They will have a church home, but their primary ministry is moving and directing those lost to the church.

Jesus was the chief evangelist. He was always on the move, preaching and teaching the kingdom of God. He came for those who are lost. Jesus's ministry was within a fifty-mile radius. He went about as the Son of Man, establishing Himself as the Son of God, who came to save the world from their sins. Among the publicans and sinners, Jesus's message was simple, and His miracles were persuasive to draw the lost to the Father in heaven. Jesus said to Zacchaeus, "For the Son of man is come to seek and to save that which was lost" (Luke 19:10).

The *euanggelion* or the message of the evangelist is simple and identifiable. Evangelists don't preach with theological terminologies.

They put the gospel in the simplest form so unbelievers can grasp and hold to the kingdom message. Evangelists will use the environment and current events to get unbelievers to see the acts of God in their lives. The Holy Spirit (by the word of God) will convict people of sins without the proclaimer pointing at the sin in their lives. The center of the evangelist's message is repentance and faith in Jesus Christ.

Jesus often used parables to teach the Gentiles the kingdom message. He used the situations at hand to illustrate God's word. In John 4, Jesus had a dialogue with a Samaritan woman at Jacob's well. Jesus used the well and water to get the woman to a level of understanding the kingdom of God message. The well and water were something the woman could relate to in her life. Jesus Christ had a revelation or a word of knowledge for the living condition and lifestyle of the woman. Therefore, He was able to get to the woman's heart. The insight Jesus had in the woman's life didn't cause Him to judge the woman, but it persuaded her to believe He was the Christ. As Jesus had passion for the publicans and sinners, the evangelist also has passion for unbelievers.

During the apostle Paul's initial visit to the Corinthians church, he preached the salvation message. The apostle Paul was spiritual and gifted, but his primary mission in establishing the church at Corinth was preaching salvation by faith in Jesus Christ. First Corinthians 2:1–2 says, "And I, brethren, when I came to you, came not with excellency of speech or of wisdom, declaring unto you the testimony of God. For I determined not to know any thing among you, save Jesus Christ, and him crucified."

Philip, an evangelist, preached the word of God in Samaria, and many heard the spoken word. The people witnessed the signs and wonders he did. Acts 8:5–7 says, "Then Philip went down to the city of Samaria, and preached Christ unto them. And the people with one accord gave heed unto those things which Philip spoke, hearing and seeing the miracles which he did; For unclean spirits, crying with a loud voice, came out of many that were possessed with them; and many taken with palsies, and that were lame, were healed."

Notice the sequence of events. Philip first preached the word of God, then the people believed what was said, then they were of one accord, and finally, miracles accompanied the preached word.

Evangelists have a way of reaching the lost through the word of God. With the help of the Holy Spirit, their message of the death, burial, and resurrection of Jesus Christ has a sense of urgency. When the people and recipients come together in one accord, ultimately they induce a corporate anointing. The Holy Spirit will move with power and heal and deliver the people from their illnesses and spiritual bondage. When evangelists operated under the anointing to do miracles, this was a confirmation to the word in which they had preached. Some people, especially those who are lost, sometimes have to see the power of God to know Jesus Christ is real.

NOTES

CHAPTER 12
The Office of the Pastor

And he gave some, apostles; and some, prophets; and
some evangelists; and some, pastors and teachers.
—Ephesians 4:11

Serving as the pastor of a local church can be the most stressful
office of the fivefold ministers. Being an overseer of God's people
takes great patience. Throughout biblical history, the overseers
of God's people had to suffer through many frustrations, stressful
situations, and anxieties. Moses was frustrated with the children of
Israel. Jesus became frustrated with the little faith of His disciples.
Paul was sometimes frustrated with the churches he'd established.
None of them gave up on the church.

To pastor a local church, one must truly love the people of
God. Over the years, a relationship develops between the pastor
and the laypeople. No one can penetrate the relationship. There
can be associate pastors in the church, but they don't have the
same kind of relationship the senior pastor has with the church.

Because of the love pastors have for the people, congregations
can have a great effect on them. Underpaid and overworked pastors
try to deal with the unrealistic expectations of their congregations.
Pastors are on call twenty-four hours a day and seven days a week.

Sometimes the weight of the constant calamities that develop in churches and in the lives of church members weighs them down.

Pastors of local churches are under great attack by the devil. If Satan can keep pastors unfocused, then the church at large won't be focused. Churches should always pray for their pastors. Pastors desire for churches to grow spiritually and numerically. Some pastors can identify with the prophet Isaiah. "I have laboured in vain, I have spent my strength for nought, and in vain" (Isa. 49:4).

Pastors counsel, teach, or preach to the people at a minimum of twice a week. They make midnight runs to visit those who face life or death situations. They console the bereaved. Then when they see there is no growth in the church, they become quite discourage and feel their effort is all for nothing. Pastors must walk by faith and not by sight. Those who walk by sight can face much discontentment. Pastors must look beyond the condition of believers and see what they can be in Christ Jesus.

So who has authority in the local church? The pastor is the only one ordained to oversee the local body. Many suggest that if the fivefold ministry isn't functioning in the local church, the church government is insufficient. Some suggest the order in which the apostle Paul gave the fivefold ministry gives one authority over the other. The arrangement Paul used (Eph. 4:11) was simply the order of ministry that first developed in the body of Christ. In the early stages of the church, there were no local churches yet established. The call of the apostle was first and then the prophet and so forth. The fact that the office of the apostle was first on the list doesn't mean he or she has authority over the flock. In all fairness, the church would benefit greatly if all five of the ministry gifts were in operation in an assembly.

When the church was in its infancy, there was only one church in Jerusalem. The apostles of Jesus preached the word there. In Acts 1:8, Jesus told His disciple they were going to witness of Him in Jerusalem, Judea, Samaria, and to the uttermost part of the earth. "But ye shall receive power, after that the Holy

Ghost is come upon you: and ye shall be witnesses unto me both in Jerusalem, and in all Judaea, and in Samaria, and unto the uttermost part of the earth" (Acts 1:8).

The church stayed in Jerusalem until the Lord allowed persecution to come. When it came, the church was scattered and went about preaching the word of God to the rest of the world. Acts 8:1 says, "And Saul was consenting unto his death. And at that time there was a great persecution against the church which was at Jerusalem; and they were all scattered abroad throughout the regions of Judaea and Samaria, except the apostles."

Those who heard the word of God and believed in Jesus Christ were scattered. They went witnessing about Jesus Christ, but the apostles remained at Jerusalem. The new work of evangelism induced the apostles to go and establish churches in the regions. Although they went abroad to preach and establish churches, their home church was in Jerusalem.

The word *pastor* is derived from the Greek word *poimen*. *Poimen* means "a shepherd or one who tends herds or flocks" (not merely one who feeds them). It is used metaphorically of Christian pastors (Eph. 4:11). Pastors guide and feed the flock.[9] The word *shepherd* comes from the same Greek word. *Episkopos* is the Greek word for "bishop and oversecr." It means "to watch or to look." An elder can also assume the position as pastor. The Greek word for *elder* is *presbuteros*. It is another term for "bishop or overseer."

The above words and definitions describe the pastoral office. We can conclude that the office of the pastor is more than just feeding the flock of God. The pastor preaches, teaches, watches over the well-being of the church, guides the church, and protects the church from any known false doctrine and attacks of the devil.

The pastoral office is a unique one. Pastors have special insight regarding the needs of the local church. They have compassion for

---

[9] W. E. Vine, Merrill F. Unger, and William White Jr, *Vine's Complete Expository Dictionary of Old and New Testament Words* (Nashville: Thomas Nelson, 1985.

the church that is different from all the other fivefold ministers. They have everyday ties to the church. If they aren't at the church, someone is calling their house with some kind of situation.

Pastors nurture the church through preaching and teaching the word of God. The main goal of pastors is maturing the saints of God to help build the kingdom of God. Pastoring is more than preaching every Sunday morning. Once individuals are in their infant stages of Christianity, pastors desire that they would grow in the Spirit. It is frustrating for pastors to see members go to church for twenty years or more but never grow up. They preach and teach so the congregation won't be tossed to and fro with every wind of doctrine. Ephesians 4:14 says, "That we henceforth be no more children, tossed to and fro, and carried about with every wind of doctrine, by the sleight of men, and cunning craftiness, whereby they lie in wait to deceive."

Many have taken scriptures out of context to establish a view or doctrine. There are men and women who haven't rightly divided the word of God and have misinterpreted the scriptures. Not everything that sounds good is good at all. Not every word that is new is a word from God. Laypeople have brought many ideas into the churches that aren't of God. Mostly the concepts are worldly or from another ministry. What may work for one ministry may not work for another. The pastor protects against such doctrines. The Lord will give the pastor a vision for the church and its community.

Some say the church is democratic; that is to say, all members have a say in the decision-making process. But there is nowhere in the scriptures where the congregation made decisions for what was best for the church. The layperson must understand that the Lord ordained, anointed, and placed pastors in their local church. The sheep follow, and the shepherd leads. But the pastor is a leader, not a dictator.

Jesus is the head of the church, the Chief Shepherd. Jesus said, "I am the good shepherd; the good shepherd giveth his life for the sheep" (John 10:11). All the pastors He called are the under shepherds. He called them, and therefore, He equips them. Pastors called by God should be sensitive to the voice and movements of the Holy Spirit. When the Holy Spirit speaks, He does so not of himself but of Jesus Christ. First Peter 5:4 says, "And when the Chief Shepherd shall appear, ye shall receive a crown of glory that fadeth not away."

The pastor is the main servant in the church. Jesus was a servant for the people. Early in Jesus's ministry, He was moved with compassion for the multitude because they were scattered abroad as sheep without a shepherd. Jesus had sympathy and ministered to the people. He preached and taught the kingdom of God. The miracles Jesus did confirmed the kingdom message and His deity as the Son of God.

Compassion is having sympathy for someone and causes one to take action to help. Matthew 9:35–36 says, "And Jesus went about all the cities and villages, teaching in they synagogues, and preaching the gospel of the kingdom, and healing every sickness and every disease among the people. But when he saw the multitudes, he was moved with compassion on them, because they fainted, and were scattered abroad as sheep having no shepherd."

The Characteristics of a Pastor

A pastor must have compassion for the people of God. Many pastors look at the office of the pastor only as a business and a position of prestige. Those who take the pastoral position for those two areas only underestimate God and have a misconception of the position. Pastors who have compassion for the church want the best for it. They care for churches and nurture them for the work of the kingdom of God. Pastors should see to local churches having balanced Christian lives.

In an effort to nurture the church, the pastor, under the guidance of the Holy Spirit, doesn't always preach what the people of God want to hear but rather what they need to hear. What the people need to hear often brings conviction to their hearts. The conviction of the Holy Spirit brings growth and deliverance to an individual and the church. Pastors shape congregations for the work of the kingdom of God. With the word of God and the help of the Holy Spirit, they will succeed. Through pastors' preaching and teaching, those in churches can live productive Christian lives for the Lord. Jesus's Sermon on the Mount taught the people to be productive and godly. Matthew 5:16 says, "Let your light so shine before men, that they may see your good works, and glorify your Father which is in heaven."

The maturing of the local church is a process. There may be healings and miracles in a moment, but Christlike character building is a growing process. Sanctification is a daily process. We should die to our flesh or worldly desires daily so we may grow spiritually and live for Christ. Church members must accept the word of God and renew their thinking to be like Christ. Before individuals were born again, we all were conformed to the world in which we live. The principle of the pastor's message is heart changing and mind transforming. Through the preaching and teaching of the pastor, the transforming word of God will prepare one to make a difference in the church, community, and world. Romans 12:1–2 says, "I beseech you therefore, brethren, by the mercies of God, that ye present your bodies a living sacrifice, holy, acceptable unto God, which is your reasonable service. And be not conformed to this world: but be ye transformed by the renewing of your mind, that ye may prove what is that good, and acceptable, and perfect, will of God."

The pastor can discipline or exalt the church too much. Too much of either can ruin the local church. The apostle Paul both exalted and disciplined the churches he established. The balance of praise and rebuking will help the people of God grow. The word of God has convictions and exaltations. People in our modern times have itching ears for a compromising gospel. The ego-stroking gospel that makes one feel good all the time doesn't lead to spiritual growth.

The Lord has given the pastor the task to nurture and train His people. The process isn't always a pleasant one. The apostle, prophet, evangelist, and teacher can minister to the people and leave, but the pastor must stay. Crusades and seminars are a form of nurturing, but they don't take the place of the pastoral duties. The pastor is the only one who has an in-depth, relational insight concerning the care of the church. He or she not only encourage the church, but also rebuke, instruct and correct. 2 Timothy 3:16 says, "All scripture is given by inspiration of God, and is profitable for doctrine, for reproof, for correction, for instruction in righteousness: That the man of God may be perfect, thoroughly furnished unto all good works."

The pastor will toil to bring unity and kingdom work ethics to the local church. Every church has its problems, and pastors must deal with them. Just as every family has its problems, so does the church. Families make up the local church; because of the various problems in churches, pastors cannot do it all by themselves. A wise pastor will use mature ministers and deacons to help with the cares of the church. Men of God who are mature in the natural and spiritual realms will accept the work of the church so pastors may give themselves to prayer and preparation for preaching the word of God and ministering to the people of God. When pastors take on too much, they can easily burn out, stress out, and become unproductive. Consequently, pastors and people of God won't be able to reach their full potential. Moses had that problem until his father-in-law came to him and suggested that he choose men of Israel and give them the authority to handle the minor things among the people (Ex. 18:13–23).

Pastors can delegate this kind of authority only to ministers and deacons of the church who are Holy Spirit filled and wise in their dealings. When pastors have Holy Spirit-filled and trustworthy ministers to help him, they can be free to meditate and prepare to minister to the church. They will be more focused on the vision the Lord gave them.

Jesus had twelve disciples who worked closely with Him, but He had more than twelve disciples. The apostle Paul had other apostles and prophets working with him. Any young minister desiring to pastor or be a leader must first learn how to be a good follower. Every young preacher must understand that not every preacher has a calling to be a pastor. Not every preacher is a teacher, although if preachers study the word of God, they will have some teaching in their sermons. Young ministers must pray and seek the Lord for their particular ministry. Pastors as overseers will help young ministers to discover their ministry. They will help nurture and develop them into what the Lord will have them do.

Pastors must remember they are sheep under Jesus Christ. They should be sensitive to the voice of the Holy Spirit to receive instruction from the Lord. We are all His sheep. Psalm 100:3 says, "Know ye that the Lord he is God: it is he that hath made us, and not we ourselves; we are his people, and the sheep of his pasture."

When pastors acknowledge that they are sheep, they stand a better chance of not getting caught up in themselves and losing their focus. As the congregation is subject to the pastor, so is the pastor subject to Christ. Christ is the head of the church. He knows what is best for the local church. There are different needs in every church and community. What may be applicable on the East Coast may not be applicable on the West Coast or in the Midwest.

Pastors should work with ministers in the other fivefold offices. This partnership doesn't take anything away from pastors, but it will enhance the spiritual growth of the church. All the ministry gift offices should have regard and appreciation for one another. Many pastors have a jealous spirit when it comes to those who operate in their respective callings. The pastor of a local church can also operate in the gifts of the Spirit. There are pastors who yield themselves to the apostolic and prophetic anointing.

Although the primary office of pastors is shepherding, they can operate in the gifts of the Holy Spirit or the other ascension gift offices or all of the above.

Pastors who understand they are the under shepherds and comprehend the movement of the Holy Spirit will have no problem with the other ministry gifts in operation. As I stated earlier, no one can penetrate or interrupt the established relationship between pastors and congregations.

There is a warning for pastors who scatter the flock of God. Throughout the Old Testament, the Lord God warned the pastors or shepherds who scattered His sheep. The Lord will bring judgment on pastors who bring division in the church, and they shall reap what they have sown. God isn't mocked: for whatsoever a man soweth, that shall he also reap, Gal. 6:7. Pastors who neglect the flock and seek to prosper themselves rather than preach and teach to the congregation shall suffer the judgment of the Lord God.

Blessed are the pastors who seek after God and feed His flock. The Lord said, "He will send pastors according to his own heart. They shall feed them with knowledge and understanding" (Jer. 4:4). Great is the reward for pastors who seek after God and nurture the church.

NOTES

CHAPTER 13
The Office of the Teacher

And he gave some, apostles; and some prophets;
and some, evangelists; and some, pastors and teachers.
—Ephesians 4:11

A teacher, like the other four offices, is a calling from Jesus Christ. Jesus Christ has placed teachers in His church. The teachers' goal is to ground believers in the word of God. Teachers help believers to be deeply rooted and established in the Lord. The Lord said, "My people are destroyed for the lack of knowledge" (Hos. 4:6). When one has the call to teach, there is a deep desire to impart knowledge and understanding to the body of Christ. Teachers are able to present both simple and complex spiritual truths. It is dangerous and life threatening for one to step into an office for which one hasn't been called or commissioned or both.

Teachers have an important role in the body of Christ. They can have a mobile or stationary ministry; they can travel throughout the city, country, or even the world, teaching the word of God. The teacher can also be stationary in one church (for example, a Sunday school teacher). The Greek word for teacher is *didaskalos*. A *didaskalos* is one who instructs or communicates knowledge.

The teachers' duty is to teach the body of Christ to understand their special relationship to Christ and to instruct them on how to serve Him with holiness and Christian character. There is a preparation process involved before there is a commission to educate others. When believers receive the call of God, they must prepare themselves by sitting under men or women who are teachers of the Holy Scriptures. There are Bible colleges and theological seminaries one should attend to help teachers rightly divide the word of truth. If nothing else, teachers should have a basic understanding of the Holy Bible. It is easy for a teacher of the word of God to become headstrong and self-righteous. Some can exalt their relationship to the church above the pastor, but that is a dangerous thing to do. Teachers communicate instructions concerning the doctrine of the Bible without assuming the role of the minister.

Not every teacher is a preacher, and not every preacher is a teacher. When believers have a dual calling to preach and teach the word of God, they have a special task in the body of Christ. Therefore, teachers must have a humble spirit to be effective teachers for Jesus Christ. The goal of teachers is to bring light to the word of God with simplicity. The office of the teacher carries the anointing to open believers' understanding to the word of God. Teachers should nurture the minds of children and adults alike. If believers serve in the office of the teacher and are unlearned, they can do more harm to the body of Christ than no teacher at all. There are teachers with the wrong spirit who go around and miseducate the church. If the material taught differs greatly from the teaching of the pastor, there is something wrong.

The Characteristics of the Teacher

Teachers are expected to demonstrate exceptional character along with their academic qualifications. They must have good organizational skills and should be able to establish a structured educational ministry. Their greatest concern is grounding the saints in proper doctrine and practical living. They should organize any educational itinerary the pastor sets.

There are teachers/apostles; teachers can have the apostolic anointing. If they are sensitive to the move of the Holy Spirit, they can experience the power of the Holy Spirit through signs, wonders, and the working of miracles. Teachers tend to rely more on their organizational skills than on their apostolic ministry.

There are teachers who are pastors, who must have compassion for the body of Christ. Pastors or teachers desire the church to grow spiritually and to modify their behavior. Like a good shepherd, they will guard the sheep against false teachers. They will be able to detect the wolves in sheep's clothing.

Teachers can operate in the prophetic anointing. If teachers are lifelong learners of the word of God, they will discover prophetic messages in the scriptures. Most prophetic messages come from the time and current environment. Therefore, teachers must be aware of current events and their surroundings. The Lord, your God, can send a prophetic word through the teacher as it pertains to a nation, the world, or an individual.

Teachers must love God and His people. When teachers love God's people, they desire to see the body of Christ prosper in spirit and in the knowledge of God. They shouldn't lock their understanding into one concept of the scriptures. The understanding of teachers is based on their studies and their natural and spiritual maturity. It is a sad commentary when teachers close their understanding and are dogmatic about their concepts of the Holy Writ. Saul had that problem until he went down the road to Damascus and met the Lord. He then had to sit under a teacher of Christ for three years. The Pharisees, Sadducees, and scribes gave Jesus trouble because their hearts were hardened against His teachings.

Teachers must have humble spirits and be even tempered. With humble spirits, they can be effective instructors for the body of Christ. Teachers who have a humble spirit are sensitive to the voice of the Holy Spirit. Teachers of the scriptures don't exalt themselves but allow the Lord to exalt them. It isn't a good practice for teachers to show how much they know; rather, they should impart understanding of the word of God. Teachers should be patient and always ready to repeat explanations. When they exalt themselves and their academics, it's easy for them to misunderstand students.

Teachers are studious. Those who operate in the office of the teacher make time to study the word of God. Teachers have good study habits and a sufficient amount of study materials. They should never get to the point where they know it all. They should be lifelong students and learners of the word of God. Instructors of the Holy Bible should have the zeal of God to know and grow. Second Timothy 2:15 says, "Study to show thyself approved unto God, a workman that needeth not to be ashamed, rightly dividing the word of truth."

Teachers are trustworthy. The Lord, your God, has entrusted the mysteries of His word in the hands of teachers. They should explain the Holy Writ with clarity and to the best of their ability. Woe to the teacher who tries to teach without preparation. Teachers should be responsible for the task pastors have assigned them to.

Teachers should be prayerful and should pray about what to teach and how to present it to the people of God. It is necessary for teachers to meet the needs of the church. They can prepare to teach on healing. However, the church may need instructions in showing love. Teachers may want to teach on one thing, but the Holy Spirit may want them to teach something else. They should be prayerful and have an awareness of the direction and directives of the Holy Spirit. Prophets and teachers at the church in Antioch were sensitive to the Holy Spirit's directives. Prophets and teachers were praying and fasting, and the Holy Spirit spoke to them and told them to separate Paul and Barnabas for the work He had called them to do. They continued fasting and praying, and they laid hands on Paul and Barnabas, sending them out to do the work of the Lord (Acts 13:1–3).

Teachers must be watchmen. This is another reason why they must be prayerful and studious. One who operates in the office of the teacher must be aware of false teachers. This must be discerned by the word of God and not by one's diagnosis or assumed idea. Jesus, Paul, Peter, and John repeatedly talked about false teachers within the church. False teachers are shrewd, subtle, and clever; their teaching sounds good and appealing, but they often point to themselves rather than to Christ. Their concepts focus on their interpretations rather than on Christ's applications. When teachers become the object of the teaching, the teaching is false as well as the teachers.

True teachers focus on Christ and His word. They lift up Jesus Christ and let Him do the drawing. True teachers don't focus on denominations, traditions, rituals, or books. The object of teaching is the person of Jesus Christ.

In light of the Old Testament and the post exile experience, the scribes were the teachers of Jewish law. They gathered themselves together to study and interpret the Torah. They preserved and interpreted the law for the conditions of the postexilic times. The prominent teacher of the Old Testament was a priest by the name of Ezra (Ezra 7).

Ezra was one of the priests who, along with Zerubbabel, led Israel back to Jerusalem after being in Babylon for seventy years. Ezra indulged himself in learning, interpreting, and exercising the word of God. He set his heart to study the word of God so he could instruct Israel in the statutes and ordinances of God (Neh. 8:2–8). Ezra was a studious and prayerful man who loved God and His people. He urged Israel to serve the Lord with their complete being, with their mouths, hearts, and minds.

In the New Testament, the prominent teacher was Jesus Christ. Our Lord taught the word of God and used parables to illustrate the kingdom of God. He used His environment as a teaching tool for life applications and faith-building tools. In Matthew 17:20, Jesus metaphorically used a mustard seed and a mountain to talk about faith. "I say unto you, If ye have faith as a grain of mustard seed, ye shall say unto this mountain, Remove hence to yonder place; and it shall remove; and nothing shall be impossible unto you."

He talked about the mustard seed, not in relation to the size of it but in regard to its quality. The mountain as an insurmountable task can be conquered if one has quality faith. The faith isn't in oneself but in Christ, who can make all things possible. Jesus had a deeper insight into the Holy Scriptures. His teachings of the scriptures weren't just surface instructions. His teachings changed the hearts and minds of the recipients. Not everyone received His teachings. We discovered that in the life of Jesus, it was the scribes (the doctors of the law) who gave Jesus trouble about His interpretation of the Holy Scriptures. Jesus's teaching dealt with the heart or the internal being of individuals.

Teachers' Methods

Good teachers will have outlines of their teaching material. Outlines will keep them on course and give direction to the presentation. Many teachers don't use an outline and end up in left field with no way back. Some teachers go to left field, using scriptures that don't relate to one another, and never finish the lesson. It's important that the lesson be completed. If a lesson cannot be finished in one segment, then a series on the lesson is sufficient.

In his writing in the New Testament, Luke had an outline or an order in which he wrote the Gospel of Luke and the book of Acts. Luke 1:3–4 says, "It seemed good to me also, having had perfect understanding of all things from the very first, to write unto thee in order, most excellent Theophilus, That thou mightest know the certainty of those things, wherein thou hast been instructed."

Luke wanted Theophilus to understand the things Jesus had done and taught. Since Luke had firsthand experience as an eyewitness, he recorded events so Theophilus could have a clear understanding of the things (Jesus) had taught. Luke brought simplicity to accounts where Theophilus had complexity. An outline gives direction and clarity to a teacher's presentation.

Effective teachers have good communication and interaction with students. Effective communication is accomplished when students hear what teachers say and understand it in the way teachers intend. The ideal situation is when teachers present their facts and information with simple and identifiable concepts. Sometimes teachers have to use visuals to get a point across, depending on the audience being addressed. Some teachers are theatrical. They use a lot of body language (for example, hand motions or movement from one side of the podium to the other) to get their point across.

The relationship between instructors and students is very important. If teachers don't have good interactions with students, students are subject not to receive the presentation of the word of God. Good teachers teach not only by precepts but also by their character, reliability, and qualifications. Teachers' conduct reinforces their precepts. Students are apt to learn if teachers live by what they are teaching.

Students learn better when there is a relationship developed between teachers and students. Jesus's disciples learned to be apostles by what He taught them. They lived with Him, and they watched the things He did. They walked with Him and listened to Him. The disciples learned through Jesus's precepts, concepts, and conduct.

One who operates in the office of the teacher will rightly divide the word of truth. Believers must live by the inspiration of the word of God and also the instructions of the scriptures. Many believers want to live by the inspirational word alone. The preached word and prophetic word are great to hear and are necessary, but there is also the instructional word of God. Every sermon prepared and preached should have some teaching in it. Those in the body of Christ like the teaching or preaching that makes them feel good, such as the teaching that talks about God's blessing, presence, and power. When the teaching calls for rebuke as well as to do something, change something, or make a sacrifice, then it doesn't meet our taste.

A good teacher can present the complexity of the scriptures with simplicity. The instructor will make it simple and identifiable. Teachers know how to take the meat of the word and turn it into milk for the new converts or babes in Christ. On the other hand, a teacher will be able to serve the meat of the word of God to those who need a deeper understanding and desire to go to higher levels. The main ideal is that a good teacher will be able to address a congregation at all particular levels.

There are four different methods of preparations for teaching. They are contextual, topical, principal, and expository.

The contextual style is a text prepared and presented in its original historical setting. The teacher will give facts and information about a text in its historical setting without any kind of spiritual or life applications. The teacher relies on the chronological, archeological discoveries and history of a certain biblical narrative. This style focuses on the intellect rather than on life and spiritual growth.

The topical style has a host of scriptures pulled together to support a subject. This is the most common style in our modern times. Topical teaching is the result of a teacher's ideal. Often this style uses scriptures out of context with no relation to one another. Teachers read different scriptures and talk about the topic with life applications. This style is applicable for scripture memorization and some life applications. Depending on the instructor, this style excites or motivates the body of Christ.

The principal style is teaching the main idea of a biblical narrative. Teachers read a story in the Holy Writ and talk about its plot. If teachers read the narrative about the woman who had an issue of blood, they would talk about the faith of the woman. Therefore, the teachers' focus would be human initiative and faith. This style has some life applications and spiritual connotations.

The expository style teaches verse by verse and line upon line. This style often gets into the meat of the word of God. The teacher will read a text and expound upon it. With this style of teaching, the teacher explores whom it was written to, why it was written, when it was written, and what was written. The teacher would make both spiritual and life applications. Depending on the text read, there can be rebuking or exhorting, if not both.

In my opinion, a teacher can be effective if all four styles are included in the presentation. The body of Christ is mixed with people on different faith and intellectual levels. If the presentation has all four styles, it stands a chance of reaching all people where they are. The word of God is for both inspiration and instruction. Second Timothy 3:16–17 says, "All Scripture is given by inspiration of God, and is profitable for doctrine, for reproof, for correction, for instruction in righteousness. That the man of God may be perfect thoroughly furnished unto all good works."

These ministry gifts are given to those the Lord has called, prepared, and ordained for the mission He has commanded to the church. Many are called into the body of Christ, but few are chosen for leadership or the fivefold ministry. Those who have accepted the call into the ascension gift ministry should receive and move at the command of the Lord. These ministries are most humble but bold in spirit for the work of the kingdom of God. Through this effort and humble disposition, the Lord God will get the glory in what we do.

There are some ministers who have gone in the way of Balaam. Woe unto them! Some apostles, prophets, evangelists, pastors, and teachers are using their gifts for reward. Some ask for monetary gifts to speak over a believer's life. The term used is "seed faith." The Lord, your God, cannot be bribed. He says obedience is better than sacrifice. Some use their gift for prestige, applause, and even power. Ministers should leave their reward in the hands of the Lord. We must remember that the pay isn't in the envelope.

The Lord was angry with Balaam, a true prophet of God. Balak wanted Balaam to curse Israel because the Israelites outnumbered the Moabites. Balaam was eager to receive the reward of Balak, the king of Moab. No matter whether the prophetic message was to curse or bless, Balaam sold out. The Lord God allowed Balaam not to curse Israel but to bless them. The result Balaam showed Balak was how he could corrupt the children of Israel (Num. 22–25). Second Peter 2:15–16 says, "Who have forsaken the right way, and are gone astray, following the way of Balaam, the son of Beor, who loved the wages of unrighteousness. But was rebuked for his iniquity; the dumb ass speaking with man's voice forbade the madness of the prophet."

EPILOGUE

The Holy Spirit is more than an influence of power, but He is able to empower us in many ways. The Holy Spirit, the Comforter, has been sent to us to empower us to carry out the mission or the great commission Jesus Christ has given us to do. The third person of the Trinity, the Holy Spirit, won't speak of Himself but of that which He hears of the Father and witness of the Christ. His will is the will of the Father. He knows the will of the Father and Christ, and He knows the heart of mankind. He was before time and the formation of the earth. "And the Spirit of God moved upon the face of the waters." Thus, He was there when Lucifer was cast out of heaven.

He knows the motives of Satan are to be like God and to destroy mankind, particularly the body of Christ; He guides and teaches us all truths. He speaks to us and gives us spiritual insight for different situations in our lives. As we further the cause of Jesus Christ, He equips us for the work of the ministry and gives us spiritual gifts as He wills. "But all these worketh that one and self-same Spirit, dividing to every man severally as He will."1 Co. 12:11

Jesus Christ gave us the ministry gifts or the fivefold ministry. "And He gave some, apostles; and some prophets; and some evangelist; and some pastors and teachers." Eph. 4:11 How long should these gifts be in place? The scripture says, "Till we all come in the unity of the faith, and the knowledge of the Son of God, unto a perfect man unto the measure of the statue of the fullness of Christ." Eph. 4:13

These gifts of the Holy Spirit and ministry gifts are the weapons of our warfare. We cannot fight the devil and his angels in our own power. We need the Holy Spirit operating in our lives then souls can be saved. Believers and unbelievers alike will be saved, delivered, and healed by the power of the Holy Spirit working through us.

Jesus said in Mark 16:17–18, "And these signs shall follow them that believe; In my name shall they cast out devils; they shall speak with new tongues; They shall take up serpents; and if they drink any deadly thing, it shall not hurt them; they shall lay hands on the sick, and they shall recover" (also see Rom. 12:5–8; 1 Cor. 12; Eph. 4:11–13).

RESOURCES

Chafer, Lewis Sperry, and John Walvoord. *Major Bible Themes.* rev. ed. Grand Rapids, MI: Zondervan, 1974.

Eckhart, John. *Moving in the Apostolic.* Ventura, CA: Renew Books, 1999.

Hagin, Kenneth E. *A Fresh Anointing.* Tulsa, OK: Rhema Bible Church, 1989.

Hagin, Kenneth E. *He Gave Gifts unto Men.* Tulsa, OK: Rhema Bible Church, 1992.

Hagin, Kenneth E. *Understanding the Anointing.* Tulsa, OK: Rhema Bible Church, 1983.

Hamon, Bill. *Apostles Prophets and the Coming Moves of God.* Shippensburg, PA: Destiny Image, 1997.

Hamon, Bill. *Prophets and Personal Prophecy; God's Prophetic Voice Today.* Shippensburg, PA: Destiny Image, 1987.

Harrison, Buddy. *Understanding Spiritual Gifts: The Operation and Administration of the Gifts of the Holy Spirit in Your Life.* Tulsa, OK: Harrison House, 1997.

Hayes, Norvel. *Endued with Power: How to Activate the Gifts of the Holy Spirit in Your Life*. Nashville: Harrison House, 1991.

McGee, Vernon J. *The Epistles Second Corinthians*. Nashville: Thomas Nelson, 1991.

Rad, Gerhard von. *The Message of the Prophets*. New York: Oliver and Boyd Ltd, HarperCollins, 1965.

Riffel, Herman. *Dream Interpretation: A Biblical Understanding*. Shippensburg, PA: Destiny Image, 1993.

Stone, Dwayne. *Gifts from the Ascended Christ: Restoring the Place of the 5-Fold Ministry*. Shippensburg, PA: Treasure House, 1999.

Sumrall, Lester. *The Gifts and Ministries of the Holy Spirit*. New Kensington, PA: Whitaker House, 1993.

Tasker, R. V. G. *2 Corinthians*, Tyndale New Testament Commentaries. Leicester, England: InterVarsity Press, 1983.

Varner, Kelley. *Corporate Anointing, Christ: Manifest in the Fullness of His Body*. Shippensburg, PA: Destiny Image, 1998.

Vine, W. E., and Merrill F. Unger. *Vine's Complete Expository Dictionary of Old and New Testament Words*. Nashville: Thomas Nelson, 1985

Wagner, Peter C. *Your Spiritual Gifts Can Help Your Church Grow*. Ventura, CA: Regal Books, 2005.

Printed in the United States
By Bookmasters